Ketogenic Diet: 60 Insanely Quick and Easy Recipes for Beginners

Jeremy Stone

Elevate Publishing Limited

TABLE OF CONTENTS

Introduction

For years we were told that fats are bad for us and, to be healthy, we should eat more carbs. But as our knowledge of science and nutrition advanced, we now know fats aren't as bad as we once thought! This is where the Ketogenic Diet comes in. Scientific studies now show the dangers and risks associated with simple carb diets. At the same time, there are many studies that show the health benefits of a high-fat, low-carb diet, including:

- **Increased Energy and Focus**

- **Increased Weight Loss**

- **Lowered Blood Sugar Levels**

- **Decreased Hunger**

- **Lowered Bad Cholesterol Levels**

- **Reduced Acne and Skin Inflammation**

Never Enough Time!

Time is the most valuable thing a man can spend.
-Theophrastus

Finding healthy and easy recipes is one of the biggest challenges you'll face when on a Ketogenic Diet. In our modern lives, we rarely have time to cook for ourselves every single day. Between work, bringing kids to practice, and cleaning up around the house, cooking healthy meals is usually the first thing to suffer. That is why it is important to have easy-to-make, Keto-friendly recipes you can use when you are on the go!

All the recipes here require fewer than 45 minutes of prep time, however most recipes can be made in only 15 minutes. Once the initial prep work is done, it's just a matter of cooking using a single skillet. You can let your meal cook while you are at work or running errands. Then when you come home you have a delicious ketogenic meal to enjoy with your family!

The book is designed to make finding the perfect recipe easy to find. The book is divided into four parts: breakfast, lunch, dinner, and snacks. Under each section, recipes are organized from the quickest total time to make to the longest. Each recipe includes full nutritional information so there's no guessing how many carbs you're eating.

Thank you for choosing 60 Days of Insanely Easy One-Skillet Recipes

You can reach me by email at elevatecan@gmail.com or on Twitter at @JeremyStoneEats

Bonus: Ketogenic Diet – How A Nutritious Low Carb Diet Will Burn Fat Fast

As a special thank you to my readers, I am giving away free copies of my book Ketogenic Diet – How A Nutritious Low-Carb Keto Diet Will Burn Fat Fast! Get over 30 quick and easy to make Keto recipes designed specifically for busy people like you. You will get awesome recipes for breakfast, lunch, dinner, and snacks with full nutritional information.

To get instant access to this book and more awesome resources, check out:

http://www.shortcuttoketosis.com/Ketogenic Guide

As an added bonus, subscribers will be given a chance to get exclusive sneak peaks of upcoming books and a chance to get **free** copies with no strings attached. **Don't worry,** we treat your e-mail with the respect it deserves. You won't get any spammy emails!!

A Quick Overview of the Ketogenic Diet

Have you ever wanted to have more energy in your day, feel better and look better? Many people have found a way to achieve a better life with a simple diet. I know, it sounds too good to be true. Yet, it really is possible to gain more energy, feel better and look better by changing the way you eat. There is no magic pill, rather it is as simple as developing an eating plan that gives your body the nutrients it needs.

What is this magic eating plan? It is known as a Ketogenic Diet. This method of eating is not so new and has been around for thousands of years. Unfortunately, modern society is selecting convenience foods generally loaded with carbohydrates and refined sugars. Today, eating is often done on the run.

Convenience is what sells and manufacturers satisfy consumers' demands. These convenience foods come with preservatives, dyes, added refined sugar, salt, and processed grains. While it may be convenient to our schedule, these foods are not convenient for our body to process.

The Ketogenic Diet may sound complex and technical; but simply put, this diet is feeding your body foods that it can process more easily. The human body is made to function using food for fuel, which in turn gives us energy. The Ketogenic Diet optimizes this process with the result of giving us more energy. There are four sources of fuel for the body: carbohydrates, fats, proteins, and ketones.

But what are ketones? Ketones occur when fat in the body is broken down. The result of a Ketogenic Diet is that fat and ketones become the main source of fuel for the body. The key to eating a Ketogenic Diet is to consume more fats, some protein and little carbohydrates. This allows the body to be in a state of nutritional ketosis.

Before starting any diet, you need to discuss the benefits/risks with your doctor. It is important to understand the impact a diet may have on your body and your medical conditions. This will help you choose a diet that will be safe and give optimal results.

Eating a Ketogenic Diet is not just eating a low carbohydrate diet. Rather than counting carbohydrates, consider being aware of your body and how it is responding to the foods you consume. Are you giving yourself the nutrients that you need? A Ketogenic Diet is a change in both lifestyle and mindset.

When the body uses carbohydrates to convert glucose to energy, blood sugar levels can drop fast. The results are hunger and cravings for sugar and carbohydrates. On a Ketogenic Diet, drops in blood sugar are minimized. This is because fats and ketones serve as fuel rather than quick-burning carbohydrates.

Weight loss is hindered by foods that cause cravings for sugar, salt and fats. These addictive foods cause over-consumption of food that never give a true feeling of satisfaction. Most often, processed foods are the culprits. On a Ketogenic Diet, these foods can be avoided as well as the resulting junk food cravings and hunger. Instead of calorie counting, stick to foods found in nature whose names are simple to pronounce.

Foods such as grains, dairy and refined sugar cause inflammation in the body. Inflammation hinders weight loss and causes toxins to build up in your body. After starting the Ketogenic Diet, the toxins will be removed and inflammation will decrease.

The above is an overview of the Ketogenic Diet. If you would like to learn more I have a beginner's guide to the Ketogenic Diet where I go more in-depth with the mechanics of the diet and give you proven strategies to help you lose weight for good.

With **Shortcut To Ketosis: Lose Weight, Feel Great!** You will also learn...

- Awesome Shortcuts to enter Ketosis
- Over 100 Quick and Easy Recipes for All Meals - Breakfast, Lunch, Dinner and Snacks
- Over 50 Full Color Pictures
- Macro and Micro Nutritional Information for Each Recipe!

Get your copy at Amazon here:
http://www.shortcuttoketosis.com/LoseWeightFeelGreat

Benefits Of One-Skillet Cooking

Time is precious, waste it wisely.

Having a good skillet is one of the must-have tools when you're on a Ketogenic Diet. Thankfully most people have at least one go-to skillet in their kitchen which makes these recipes so easy that everyone can use them. These are some of my favourite recipes, not only because they taste good, but because I like quick and easy meals so I can focus my time on family and friends. Here are some more benefits of one-skillet cooking:

More nutrient rich food - When you cook at home instead of eating out, you know exactly what you're putting into your system and you can get much more nutrient-rich food. For example, if a recipe calls for butte,r always opt for grass-fed butter, as it has more Omega 3's and antioxidant vitamins.

Saves money – Not only do you get more nutrient rich food by cooking at home, but you also save money by not eating out. A $15-$20 meal may not seem like a lot at first, but it can add up if you get 3-4 meals at the same price.

Less clean up - Since you're only using one skillet to make your food, the time you spend on cleaning up will be much less than with conventional methods.

Saves time – Most recipes in this book take less than 30 minutes in total to make. Even if you were to go out and buy fast food, it would probably take less time to make one of these recipes than it would to go out and come back.

Breakfast

Cheesy Salsa Omelet

Prep Time: 05 minutes   **Cook Time:** 05 minutes

Serving Size: 150 g   **Serves:** 2

Calories: 312; **Total Fat:** 27.5 g

Saturated Fat: 7.7 g; **Trans Fat:** 0 g

Protein: 15.1 g

Total Carbs: 2.9 g; **Net Carbs:** 2.4 g

Dietary Fiber: 0.5 g; **Sugars:** 1.7 g

Cholesterol: 342 mg; **Sodium:** 484 mg

Potassium: 230 mg; **Iron:** 10%

Vitamin A: 14%; **Vitamin C:** 01%; **Calcium:** 16%;

Ingredients:
- ☐ 4 eggs
- ☐ 1/4 cup salsa
- ☐ 1/4 cup cheddar cheese, low fat
- ☐ 1 teaspoon fresh cilantro, chopped
- ☐ Dash ground black pepper
- ☐ Dash salt
- ☐ 2 tablespoon olive oil

Directions:
1. In a small bowl, whisk the eggs together. Season with a dash of salt and pepper.

2. Grease the skillet with the olive oil. Place over medium heat.
3. Pour in the whisked eggs. Cook for about 2-3 minutes, lifting the edges to spread the uncooked egg.
4. Sprinkle the cheese over the cooking egg. Place the lid of the skillet. Cook for about 2 minutes or until the egg is cooked through and the cheese is melted. Carefully fold the omelet in half. Cut into pieces. Remove from the skillet. Garnish each serving with the salsa and the cilantro.

Furikake-Spiced Eggs and Asparagus

Prep Time: 05 minutes   **Cook Time:** 05 minutes

Serving Size: 274 g   **Serves:** 1

Calories: 412; **Total Fat:** 36.2 g

Saturated Fat: 19.3 g; **Trans Fat:** 0 g

Protein: 16 g

Total Carbs: 10.4 g; **Net Carbs:** 6.3 g

Dietary Fiber: 4.1 g; **Sugars:** 3.5 g

Cholesterol: 438 mg; **Sodium:** 306 mg

Potassium: 475 mg; **Iron:** 28%

Vitamin A: 46%; **Vitamin C:** 27%; **Calcium:** 13%

Ingredients:

- ☐ 2 tablespoon ghee
- ☐ 8 thin asparagus stalks, trimmed
- ☐ 2 large eggs
- ☐ Freshly ground black pepper
- ☐ Kosher salt
- ☐ 1/2 lemon, juice
- ☐ 1 tablespoon furikake seasoning

Directions:

1. Arrange the oven rack about 4-6 inches from the heating source. Preheat the broiler.
2. In an 8-inch cast iron skillet, heat the ghee over high heat. When ghee is sizzling, remove the skillet

from the heat. Toss the asparagus into the skillet. Gently shake to coat the spears with the ghee.

3. Crack the eggs next to the spears. Season with salt and pepper to taste.
4. Place the skillet under the broiler for about 1-2 minutes, cooking the eggs to your desired doneness.
5. Remove the skillet from the broiler. Season with lemon juice.
6. Sprinkle the spears and eggs liberally with furikake.

Mexican Cheese Scramble

Prep Time: 05 minutes   **Cook Time:** 05 minutes

Serving Size: 127 g **Serves**: 4	
Calories: 248; **Total Fat:** 20.1 g	
Saturated Fat: 9.8 g; **Trans Fat**: 0 g	
Protein: 14.9 g	
Total Carbs: 2.5 g; **Net Carbs:** 2.5 g	
Dietary Fiber: 0 g; **Sugars:** 1.9 g	
Cholesterol: 361 mg; **Sodium**: 553 mg	
Potassium: 182 mg; **Iron**: 10%	
Vitamin A: 14%; **Vitamin C**: 01%; **Calcium**: 16%	

Ingredients:

- ☐ 8 eggs, large
- ☐ 4 tablespoons salsa
- ☐ 1/4 teaspoon salt
- ☐ 1/4 teaspoon pepper, black
- ☐ 1/2 cup Mexican blend cheese, low fat
- ☐ 2 tablespoons olive oil

Directions:

1. In a small bowl, whisk the eggs together. Add in the salt and the pepper. Mix well.
2. Grease a non-stick skillet with the olive oil. Place over medium heat.
3. Pour the eggs into the skillet, stirring occasionally.
4. Top with cheese. Allow to melt. Serve with salsa.

Smoked Salmon Egg Scramble

Prep Time: 05 minutes   **Cook Time:** 05 minutes

Serving Size: 118 g **Serves**: 4	
Calories: 257; **Total Fat:** 22.3 g	
Saturated Fat: 7.9 g; **Trans Fat**: 0 g	
Protein: 14.1 g	
Total Carbs: 1.2 g; **Net Carbs:** 1.2 g	
Dietary Fiber: 0 g; **Sugars:** 0.6 g	
Cholesterol: 278 mg; **Sodium:** 312 mg	
Potassium: 201 mg; **Iron**: 09%	
Vitamin A: 14%; **Vitamin C**: 06%; **Calcium**: 02%	

Ingredients:

- ☐ 6 eggs, large
- ☐ 3 ounces salmon, smoked, cut into small bite-sized pieces
- ☐ 3 ounces cream cheese, 1/3 less fat, cut into small pieces
- ☐ 2 tablespoons fresh chives, chopped, snipped
- ☐ 1/4 teaspoon salt
- ☐ 1/4 teaspoon black pepper
- ☐ 2 tablespoon olive oil

Directions:

1. Grease a large non-stick skillet with the olive oil. Place over medium heat.

2. In a small mixing bowl, whisk the eggs, salt, and pepper together.
3. Pour the egg mixture into and skillet and scramble lightly until half-way cooked.
4. Add in the salmon and the cream cheese. Just barely mix into the eggs. Serve topped with chives.

Denver Omelet

Prep Time: 05 minutes   **Cook Time:** 10 minutes

Serving Size: 154 g   **Serves:** 4

Calories: 258; **Total Fat:** 20.4 g

Saturated Fat: 5.8 g; **Trans Fat:** 0 g

Protein: 15.7 g

Total Carbs: 3.9 g; **Net Carbs:** 2.8 g

Dietary Fiber: 1.1 g; **Sugars:** 1.9 g

Cholesterol: 344 mg; **Sodium:** 481 mg

Potassium: 234 mg; **Iron:** 13%

Vitamin A: 23%; **Vitamin C:** 28%; **Calcium:** 12%

Ingredients:

- ☐ 8 olives, black, pitted, chopped
- ☐ 8 eggs, large
- ☐ 2 ounces ham, lean, sliced
- ☐ 3 green onions, chopped
- ☐ 1/4 cup Mexican blend cheese, low fat
- ☐ 1/2 red pepper (or any color), seeded, chopped
- ☐ 1 tablespoon parsley, chopped
- ☐ 2 tablespoons olive oil

Direction:

1. In a medium mixing bowl, beat the eggs together.
2. Grease a large non-stick skillet with cooking spray. Place over medium heat

3. Put in the peppers. Cook for about 3 minutes or until soft.
4. Add in the ham, black olives, and green onions. Stir and spread out evenly.
5. Pour the egg mixture over, covering the vegetables. Cook for about 2 minutes or until the eggs are cooked through. Top with grated cheese. Cut into for wedges. Serve.

Peppery Eggs with Sausage

Prep Time: 05 minutes   **Cook Time:** 10 minutes

Serving Size: 220 g **Serves**: 2	
Calories: 448; **Total Fat:** 38 g	
Saturated Fat: 10.9 g; **Trans Fat**: 0.1 g	
Protein: 21.5 g	
Total Carbs: 6.2 g; **Net Carbs:** 4.6 g	
Dietary Fiber: 1.6 g; **Sugars:** 4.3 g	
Cholesterol: 330 mg; **Sodium:** 587 mg	
Potassium: 386 mg; **Iron**: 13%	
Vitamin A: 46%; **Vitamin C:** 129%; **Calcium**: 15%	

Ingredients:

- ☐ 3 turkey sausage breakfast links (about 3 ounces), casings removed, cut into small pieces.
- ☐ 3 large eggs
- ☐ 1 ounce jack or Mexican blend cheese, reduced fat
- ☐ 1/4 red onion, chopped
- ☐ 1 red bell pepper (or any color), seeded, chopped
- ☐ 1 teaspoon chives, for garnish
- ☐ Salt and pepper, to taste
- ☐ 2 tablespoons olive oil

Directions:

1. Grease a medium non-stick skillet with the olive oil. Place over medium heat.

2. Put the sausage into the skillet. Cook until brown.
3. Add in the onions. Stir.
4. Add in the pepper. Cook for about 2 minutes, occasionally stirring.
5. When the sausages are cooked through and the vegetables are soft, move to the side of the skillet.
6. In a small bowl, whisk the eggs together. Pour the whisked egg into the empty side of the skillet. Adjust heat to medium low. Cook for about 1 minute.
7. Mix the sausage, vegetables, and the eggs. Cook until the eggs are just done.
8. Top with chives and cheese. Serve.

Asparagus Frittata

Prep Time: 05 minutes	**Cook Time:** 15 minutes

Serving Size: 216 g   **Serves:** 2
Calories: 267; **Total Fat:** 22.1 g
Saturated Fat: 5.6 g; **Trans Fat:** 0 g
Protein: 14.4 g
Total Carbs: 5.4 g; **Net Carbs:** 3 g
Dietary Fiber: 2.4 g; **Sugars:** 2.8 g
Cholesterol: 175 mg; **Sodium:** 163 mg
Potassium: 357 mg; **Iron:** 19%
Vitamin A: 31%; **Vitamin C:** 11%; **Calcium:** 13%

Ingredients:

- ☐ 1/2 pound asparagus, fresh or frozen, tough ends removed
- ☐ 1/4 teaspoon garlic powder
- ☐ 2 eggs, large
- ☐ 2 egg whites, large
- ☐ 3 tablespoons cheddar cheese, reduced fat, thinly shredded
- ☐ 2 tablespoons olive oil

To taste:

- ☐ Salt and pepper

Directions:

1. Preheat broiler.
2. Over medium heat, grease a non-stick skillet with the olive oil.
3. Put in the asparagus. Cook for about 3 minutes, stirring occasionally, until crisp-tender. Arrange in a single layer in the skillet.
4. In a small mixing bowl, whisk the eggs, egg whites, and the garlic powder together. Pour over the asparagus in the skillet. Sprinkle with the cheddar cheese.
5. Transfer the skillet, placing it under the broiler. Broil for about 1-2 minutes or until the eggs are cooked through. Remove from the broiler and slightly cool before serving.

Green Eggs and Mushrooms

Prep Time: 10 minutes	**Cook Time:** 10 minutes

Serving Size: 178 g	**Serves:** 4

Calories: 291; **Total Fat:** 24 g

Saturated Fat: 7.2 g; **Trans Fat:** 0 g

Protein: 16.2 g

Total Carbs: 3.9 g; **Net Carbs:** 3.1 g

Dietary Fiber: 0.8 g; **Sugars:** 1.8 g

Cholesterol: 342 mg; **Sodium:** 373 mg;

Potassium: 418 mg; **Iron:** 13%

Vitamin A: 40%; **Vitamin C:** 08%; **Calcium:** 17%

Ingredients:

- ☐ 6 ounces Cremini or button or combination mushrooms, chopped
- ☐ 8 eggs, large
- ☐ 2 cups fresh baby spinach, chopped
- ☐ 1/4 teaspoon salt
- ☐ 1/4 teaspoon black pepper
- ☐ 1/4 red onion, chopped
- ☐ 1/2 cup cheddar cheese, low fat, shredded
- ☐ 3 tablespoons olive oil

Directions:

1. In a medium whisking bowl, beat the eggs, salt, and pepper together.
2. Grease a large non-stick skillet with the olive oil.
3. Put the onions and the mushrooms. Sauté for about 3 minutes, occasionally stirring.

4. Add the spinach. Cook for about 1 minute or until wilted.
5. Push the vegetables to one side of the skillet.
6. Add more cooking spray into the skillet.
7. Pour the eggs on the empty skillet side. Cook for about 3 minutes, occasionally stirring.
8. When the eggs are done, combine with the vegetables. Top with the cheese. Serve.

Cream Cheese Cinnamon Pancakes

Prep Time: 05 minutes   **Cook Time:** 15 minutes

Serving Size: 37 g **Serves:** 4	
Calories: 87; **Total Fat:** 7.1 g	
Saturated Fat: 3.8 g; **Trans Fat**: 0 g	
Protein: 3.8 g	
Total Carbs: 1.8 g; **Net Carbs:** 1.8 g	
Dietary Fiber: 0 g**; Sugars:** 1.2 g	
Cholesterol: 97 mg; **Sodium**: 73 mg	
Potassium: 48 mg; **Iron:** 3%	
Vitamin A: 6%; **Vitamin C**: 0%; **Calcium:** 3%	

Ingredients:

- ☐ 2 ounces cream cheese
- ☐ 2 large eggs
- ☐ 1/2 teaspoon cinnamon
- ☐ 1 tsp Splenda

Directions:

1. Put all of the ingredients in the blender. Blend until the mixture is smooth. Let rest for about 2 minutes to settle the bubbles.
2. Pour 1/4 of the batter into a greased non-stick skillet. Cook for about 2 minutes or until golden. Flip and then cook for 1 minute more. Repeat the process with the remaining batter.
3. Serve with sugar-free syrup and fresh berries.

Italian Frittata

Prep Time: 10 minutes   **Cook Time:** 15 minutes

Serving Size: 416 g   **Serves:** 4

Calories: 408; **Total Fat:** 33.1 g

Saturated Fat: 8.0 g; **Trans Fat**: 0 g

Protein: 17.7 g

Total Carbs: 14.1 g; **Net Carbs:** 10.4 g

Dietary Fiber: 3.7 g; **Sugars:** 8.0 g

Cholesterol: 299 mg; **Sodium:** 238 mg

Potassium: 949 mg; **Iron:** 14%

Vitamin A: 49%; **Vitamin C**: 116%; **Calcium:** 20%

Ingredients:

- 8 ounces Cremini or button or combination mushrooms, sliced
- 7 eggs, large
- 2 zucchini or yellow squash, halved, sliced
- 2 tablespoons parmesan cheese, grated
- 14 ounces tomatoes, canned with Italian seasoning, drained
- 1/4 teaspoon garlic powder
- 1/2 large onion, chopped
- 1 red bell pepper (or any color), cored, seeded, chopped
- 1 ounce light cheddar cheese, shredded
- 6 tablespoons olive oil
- Ground black pepper, to taste

Directions:

1. Preheat the broiler.
2. Grease an oven-safe non-stick skillet with the cooking spray. Place over medium heat.
3. Put in the onions, mushrooms, zucchini, and pepper. Cook for about 4 minutes or until soft, occasionally stirring.
4. Add the garlic powder. Stir and then spread the vegetables in an even layer in the skillet.
5. Add the drained tomatoes in patches over the skillet.
6. In a bowl, whisk the eggs together. Pour over the vegetables. Reduce heat to low. Cook for about 1 minute. Transfer the skillet into the broiler. Broil for about 2 minutes or until the eggs are cooked through.
7. Sprinkle the cheddar cheese over the eggs. Return to the broiler. Broil for another 30 seconds.
8. Garnish with grated parmesan cheese, black pepper, and green onions or parsley, if desired. Serve.

Egg Sausage Guacamole Muffin

Prep Time: 15 minutes   **Cook Time:** 20 minutes

Serving Size: 313 g **Serves**: 1	
Calories: 773; **Total Fat:** 69.6 g	
Saturated Fat: 29.5 g; **Trans Fat**: 0.3 g	
Protein: 34.9 g	
Total Carbs: 1.8 g; **Net Carbs:** 1.3 g	
Dietary Fiber: 0.5 g; **Sugars:** 1.0 g	
Cholesterol: 533 mg; **Sodium:** 1190 mg	
Potassium: 471 mg; **Iron**: 19%	
Vitamin A: 26%; **Vitamin C**: 01%; **Calcium**: 07%	

Ingredients:

- 2 large eggs
- 2 tablespoons ghee, divided (plus more for greasing biscuit cutters)
- 1/4 pound raw pork breakfast sausage
- 1/4 cup water
- 1 tablespoon guacamole, heaping
- Freshly ground black pepper
- Kosher salt

Directions:
For the eggy bun:

1. Into 2 small bowls, crack 1 egg into each. With a fork, pierce the yolks.
2. Grease the insides of 2 stainless steel, round 3 ½-inch biscuit cutters.

3. In a skillet with a tight-fitting lid, heat 1 tablespoon of the ghee over medium-high heat.
4. When the ghee is shimmering. Place the biscuit cutters in the pan. Pour an egg into each cutter. Season with salt and pepper to taste. Carefully pour the 1/4 cup of water into the skillet outside the biscuit cutters, making sure the water does not splash into the eggs. Turn the heat to low. Cover the skillet. Cook the eggs for about 3 minutes or until cooked through. When cooked, transfer the eggs into a paper-lined plate.

For the patty:
1. Clean the biscuit cutter and grease it well with ghee again.
2. Place one cutter on a plate. Fill it with the sausage meat. Gently press the meat to form a sausage patty shape.
3. Pour the water out from the skillet. Heat until the water evaporates completely. Add the remaining 1 tablespoon of ghee. When the ghee is shimmering, add the patty into the skillet. If you want a perfectly round shaped patty, keep the mold until the patty shrinks away from the sides, and then remove it.
4. Fry the sausage for about 2-3 minutes per side or until thoroughly cooked. If the patty is thick, you may have to cover the pan with the lid until it is cooked through.
5. When cooked, place on top of an egg bun. Top the patty with guacamole, spreading it even over the patty. Top with the other egg bun. Enjoy!

Artichoke Frittata

Prep Time: 10 minutes   **Cook Time:** 30 minutes

Serving Size: 135 g   **Serves:** 6

Calories: 228; **Total Fat:** 19.1 g

Saturated Fat: 4.3 g; **Trans Fat**: 0 g

Protein: 10.3 g

Total Carbs: 6.4 g; **Net Carbs:** 3.9 g

Dietary Fiber: 2.5 g; **Sugars:** 1.6 g

Cholesterol: 116 mg; **Sodium**: 376 mg

Potassium: 291 mg; **Iron**: 07%

Vitamin A: 11%; **Vitamin C**: 29%; **Calcium**: 12%

Ingredients:

- 4 eggs, large
- 3 egg whites, large
- 1 cup artichoke hearts, canned, chopped
- 1/4 teaspoon black pepper, ground
- 1/4 onion, medium, chopped finely
- 1/4 cup parmesan cheese, grated
- 1/2 teaspoon salt
- 1/2 teaspoon garlic powder
- 1/2 red pepper, or any color
- 1 cup mushrooms, button or Cremini or combination, sliced
- 6 tablespoons olive oil

Directions:
1. Preheat broiler.
2. Grease a large skillet with the olive oil. Heat over medium heat.
3. Put in the onions and red pepper. Stir, cooking for about 2-minutes.
4. Add in the mushrooms. Stir, cooking for about 1 minute.
5. Add in the artichoke hearts. Stir everything together.
6. In a medium mixing bowl, whisk the eggs and the egg whites together. Season with the garlic powder, salt, and pepper. Whisk again.
7. Pour the egg mixture over the vegetables in the skillet.
8. Place the cover of the skillet. Reduce heat to low. Continue cooking for about 5 minutes, or until the eggs are set. Sprinkle with the parmesan cheese.
9. Transfer skillet into the broiler. Broil for about 2-3 minutes or until the eggs are thoroughly cooked and the cheese is slightly bubbly.
10. Cut into 6 wedges. Carefully remove each wedge with a spatula. Serve.

Canadian Bacon-y Brussels Sprouts

Prep Time: 15 minutes   **Cook Time:** 25 minutes

Serving Size: 138 g   **Serves:** 6

Calories: 96; **Total Fat:** 4.2 g

Saturated Fat: 0.8 g; **Trans Fat:** 0 g

Protein: 6.1 g

Total Carbs: 11.7 g; **Net Carbs:** 7.2 g

Dietary Fiber: 4.5 g; **Sugars:** 2.9 g

Cholesterol: 5 mg; **Sodium:** 312 mg

Potassium: 494 mg; **Iron:** 09%

Vitamin A: 17%; **Vitamin C:** 161%; **Calcium:** 04%

Ingredients:

- 2 ounces Canadian bacon, chopped
- 1 ½ pounds Brussels sprouts, trimmed, quartered
- 1/2 large onion, chopped
- 1 teaspoon sesame oil, dark
- 1 teaspoon garlic, bottled, minced
- 1 tablespoon soy sauce, low sodium
- 1 tablespoon olive oil

Directions:

1. Pour the olive oil in the skillet. Place the pan over medium or medium high heat.
2. Put in the onions. Add a dash of salt. Stir, cooking for about 1 minute.

3. Add in the Brussels sprouts. Cook for about 5 minutes, occasionally stirring.
4. Add in the remaining ingredients. Stir to combine. Cook for about 2-3 minutes or until tender.

Green Eggs with Yogurt and Chili Oil

Prep Time: 15 minutes   **Cook Time:** 25 minutes

Serving Size: 171 g   **Serves:** 2-4

Calories: 222; **Total Fat:** 18.5 g

Saturated Fat: 6.6 g; **Trans Fat**: 0 g

Protein: 10.9 g

Total Carbs: 5.4 g; **Net Carbs:** 3.3 g

Dietary Fiber: 2.1 g; **Sugars:** 1.9 g

Cholesterol: 202 mg; **Sodium**: 218 mg

Potassium: 548 mg; **Iron**: 18%

Vitamin A: 153%; **Vitamin C**: 03%; **Calcium**: 14%

Ingredients:

- ☐ 1 ¼ cups fresh spinach
- ☐ 4 large eggs
- ☐ 3 tablespoons leek, chopped (pale green and white parts only)
- ☐ 2/3 cup of plain Greek yogurt
- ☐ 2 tablespoons unsalted butter, divided
- ☐ 2 tablespoons olive oil
- ☐ 2 tablespoons scallion, chopped pale green and white parts only
- ☐ 1/4 teaspoon red pepper flakes, crushed + a pinch of paprika
- ☐ 1 teaspoon fresh lemon juice
- ☐ 1 teaspoon fresh oregano, chopped
- ☐ 1 garlic clove, halved

☐ Kosher salt

Directions:
1. In a small bowl, mix the yogurt, garlic, and a pinch of salt together. Set aside.
2. Preheat oven to 300F.
3. In an oven-safe 10-inch skillet, melt 1 tablespoon of the butter. Add in the red pepper flakes, and the paprika, cook for about 1-2 minutes until brown bits appear in the bottom. Add in the oregano. Cook for 30 seconds more. Transfer to a bowl. Set aside.
4. In the same skillet, melt the remaining 1 tablespoon of the butter over medium heat.
5. Put in the scallion and the leek. Reduce heat to low. Cook for about 10 minutes or until the vegetables are soft.
6. Add the spinach and pour the lemon juice. Season with kosher salt. Increase the heat to medium high. Cook for about 4-5 minutes, or until the spinach is wilted. Drain the excess liquid.
7. Make 4 deep holes in the mixture. Carefully break 1 egg into each hole, making sure the yolks stay intact. Transfer the skillet into the oven. Bake for about 10-15 minutes or until the egg whites are set.
8. Remove the garlic from the yogurt and discard.
9. Spoon the yogurt over the spinach and eggs. Drizzle with the spiced butter.

Brussels Sprouts Egg Burgers

Prep Time: 35 minutes   **Cook Time:** 10 minutes

Serving Size: 143 g   **Serves:** 12

Calories: 300; **Total Fat:** 24.9 g

Saturated Fat: 6.7 g; **Trans Fat**: 0 g

Protein: 13.8 g

Total Carbs: 7.1 g; **Net Carbs:** 5.1 g

Dietary Fiber: 2.0 g; **Sugars:** 1.4 g

Cholesterol: 338 mg; **Sodium**: 158 mg

Potassium: 228 mg; **Iron**: 14%

Vitamin A: 15%; **Vitamin C**: 3208%; **Calcium**: 07%

Ingredients:

- 3 cups of Brussels sprouts, cleaned well
- 24 eggs
- 1/2 teaspoon white pepper
- 1/2 cup cream cheese
- 1/2 cup spring onions, chopped
- 1/2 cup black bean flour, Gluten free
- 3/4 cup olive oil

Directions:

1. In a non-stick skillet, fry 1 egg at a time. This will serve as the burger buns. When cooked, transfer the eggs into a paper-lined plate.
2. Put the Brussels sprouts and process in the food processor.

3. In a large mixing bowl, mix the Brussels sprouts, black bean flour, cream cheese, eggs, spring onion, and the white pepper. Form into small patties, about the size of the egg buns.
4. In the same skillet used to fry the egg buns, cook the patties for about 3 minutes each side, or until crispy. Sandwich between 2 egg buns.

Pumpkin Pancakes

Prep Time: 40 minutes   **Cook Time:** 15 minutes

Serving Size: 73 g   **Serves:** 12

Calories: 185; **Total Fat:** 17.3 g

Saturated Fat: 11.1 g; **Trans Fat:** 0 g

Protein: 4.1 g

Total Carbs: 4.2 g; **Net Carbs:** 3.0 g

Dietary Fiber: 1.2 g; **Sugars:** 1.9 g

Cholesterol: 83 mg; **Sodium:** 131 mg

Potassium: 117 mg; **Iron:** 10%

Vitamin A: 75%; **Vitamin C:** 02%; **Calcium:** 04%

Ingredients:

- ☐ 1 ½ cups of cream cheese
- ☐ 1 cup pumpkin puree
- ☐ 1 cup coconut flour
- ☐ 3 eggs
- ☐ 2 teaspoon Stevia
- ☐ 1/2 teaspoon chili flakes
- ☐ 1/3 teaspoon pumpkin spice
- ☐ 1/4 cup butter, melted

Directions:

1. In a large bowl, whisk the pumpkin puree, coconut flour, cream cheese, eggs, stevia, pumpkin spice, chili flakes, and melted butter. Mix well. Let rest covered for about 15 minutes.

2. Heat a non-stick skillet. When hot, pour a ladle of the pancake mixture. Reduce heat. Cook pancake for about 2 minutes. Flip and cook more until fluffy and golden. Serve hot with a dab of butter.

Lunch

Seared Salmon with Avocado Aioli

Prep Time: 10 minutes   **Cook Time:** 10 minutes

Serving Size: 262 g   **Serves:** 4

Calories: 330; **Total Fat:** 30 g

Saturated Fat: 5 g; **Trans Fat:** 0.1 g

Protein: 8 g

Total Carbs: 11 g; **Net Carbs:** 5 g

Dietary Fiber: 6 g; **Sugars:** 1.0 g

Cholesterol: 20 mg; **Sodium:** 420 mg

Potassium: 460 mg; **Iron:** 15%

Calcium: 02%; **Vitamin C:** 30%; **Calcium:** 06%

Ingredients:
For the salmon:
- [ ] 4-ounce salmon fillet, per person
- [ ] Olive oil
- [ ] Salt
- [ ] Pepper

For the aioli:
- [ ] 1 avocado, peeled and pit removed
- [ ] 1/4 cup Greek yogurt
- [ ] 2 cloves garlic
- [ ] Juice of 1/2 lemon
- [ ] 1/4 cup olive oil
- [ ] Salt and pepper, to taste

Directions:
1. Rinse and then pat the salmon dry using paper towel.
2. Coat the fillets with the olive oil and then season both sides with the salt and pepper.
3. Heat olive oil in a skillet. Add the salmon fillets; cook for 4 to 5 minutes, or until seared. Flip, turn the heat off; let sit in the skillet for about 1 to 2 minutes, or until flaked easily using a fork.
4. Meanwhile, blend all of the aioli ingredients in a food processor for 1 minute or until the mixture is creamy.
5. Serve the salmon topped with the aioli.

Cajun Grilled Salmon

Prep Time: 05 minutes	**Cook Time:** 10 minutes

Serving Size: 142 g   **Serves:** 4

Calories: 306; **Total Fat:** 24.6 g

Saturated Fat: 3.5 g; **Trans Fat:** 0 g

Protein: 22.4 g

Total Carbs: 1.4 g; **Net Carbs:** 0.9 g

Dietary Fiber: 0.5 g; **Sugars:** 0 g

Cholesterol: 50mg; **Sodium:** 350 mg

Potassium: 494 mg; **Iron:** 06%

Vitamin A: 18%; **Vitamin C:** 04%; **Calcium:** 05%

Ingredients:

- ☐ 3/4 cups of fresh baby spinach
- ☐ 1 ½ pounds wild salmon, steaks or filet
- ☐ 1/2 teaspoon salt
- ☐ 1/2 teaspoon black pepper, ground
- ☐ 1/2 teaspoon onion powder
- ☐ 1/2 teaspoon garlic powder
- ☐ 1/2 teaspoon chili powder
- ☐ 1 teaspoon brown sugar, packed (1/2-1 packet stevia)
- ☐ 1 tablespoon olive oil
- ☐ 1 lemon, for garnish

Directions:

1. In a small bowl, combine the garlic powder, onion powder, chili powder, sugar, salt, and pepper. Mix all the ingredients well.
2. In a large skillet, heat the olive oil over medium or medium-high heat.
3. Put the salmon in the hot skillet. Sear each side without moving for about 3-4 minutes. Depending on the thickness of the fish, you may have to lower to heat and then cover the skillet, adjusting the heat to low and cooking for 1-2 minutes more until desired doneness.
4. Transfer into a plate with a bed of spinach. Garnish with lemon. Serve.

Steak Salad

Prep Time: 10 minutes   **Cook Time:** 15 minutes

Serving Size: 560 g   **Serves:** 1

Calories: 93; **Total Fat:** 75 g

Saturated Fat: 3 g; **Trans Fat:** 5 g

Protein: 7 g

Total Carbs: 10 g; **Net Carbs:** 5 g

Dietary Fiber: 6 g; **Sugars:** 1.0 g

Cholesterol: 170 mg; **Sodium:** 1450 mg

Potassium: 1290 mg; **Iron:** 20%

Vitamin A: 45%; **Vitamin C:** 45%; **Calcium:** 30%

Ingredients:

- [ ] 1 cup radicchio (optional, or your preferred veggies)
- [ ] 1 teaspoon lemon juice or white vinegar
- [ ] 1/2 teaspoon pepper freshly ground
- [ ] 1/2 teaspoon sea salt
- [ ] 2 cups arugula (or your preferred gourmet green)
- [ ] 2 Roma tomatoes, cut into chunks
- [ ] 2 tablespoons extra-virgin olive oil
- [ ] 3 tablespoon bleu cheese, crumbled (I love Maytag!)
- [ ] 6-8 ounces steak, NY strip, ribeye, cut into thin slices (or chicken)
- [ ] Canola or coconut oil, cooking spray

☐ Salt and pepper, for the steak

Directions:
1. Heat a small-sized cast-iron skillet, about 6 to 7-inch, over medium heat until hot. When hot, coat with the cooking spray. Sprinkle the steak with salt and pepper, add to the skillet, and sear until your preferred doneness. Imagine the skillet with four quadrants. Push the steak into quadrant 1.
2. Reduce the heat to medium low; add the tomatoes to quadrant 2, sprinkle with ¼ teaspoon salt and 1/4 teaspoon pepper, cover, and let steam for about 2 minutes. Add the arugula into quadrant 3, and the radicchio to quadrant 4. Cover with a lid; steam for about 90 seconds to 2 more minutes.
3. Remove the pan from the heat. Sprinkle with the remaining 1/4 teaspoon salt and 1/4 teaspoon pepper. Add the cheese and then drizzle with the olive oil and the lemon juice. Serve!

Chicken Strawberry Gorgonzola Salad

Prep Time: 10 minutes	**Cook Time:** 10 minutes
Serving Size: 268 g	**Serves:** 4

Calories: 405; **Total Fat:** 21.6 g

Saturated Fat: 3.7 g; **Trans Fat:** 5 g

Protein: 41.7 g

Total Carbs: 13.2 g; **Net Carbs:** 10.7 g

Dietary Fiber: 2.5 g; **Sugars:** 4.9 g

Cholesterol: 113 mg; **Sodium:** 426 mg

Potassium: 509 mg; **Iron:** 19%

Vitamin A: 5%; **Vitamin C:** 59%; **Calcium:** 09%

Ingredients:

- ☐ 1 pound chicken breast, boneless, skinless
- ☐ 1 bag (about 7 ounces) lettuce
- ☐ 1 ½ cups strawberries, fresh, sliced
- ☐ 1/2 teaspoon garlic powder
- ☐ 1/4 cup gorgonzola cheese (about 1 ounce)
- ☐ 1/4 cup pecans or walnuts
- ☐ 1/4 teaspoon pepper, black, ground
- ☐ 2 green onions, chopped
- ☐ 2 teaspoons olive oil

For the salad dressing:

- ☐ 2 tablespoons olive oil
- ☐ 1 teaspoon Dijon

☐ 1 teaspoon honey

☐ 1 tablespoon balsamic vinegar

Directions:

1. Cut the chicken into 1-inch thick pieces and then cut the pieces into 1-inch strips. Season with the pepper and the garlic powder.
2. Heat a large skillet over medium or medium high heat. Pour 2 tablespoons of olive oil. Put in the chicken. Brown for about 2 minutes each side or until cooked through. Remove the chicken and transfer into a plate to cool.
3. In a large salad bowl, put the lettuce and then the strawberries. Add in the chicken, onions, cheese, and the pecans.
4. In a small bowl, mix the salad dressing ingredients together. Pour over the salad. Toss gently. Serve.

Salmon with Tropical Salsa

Prep Time: 10 minutes   **Cook Time:** 10 minutes

Serving Size: 241 g   **Serves:** 6

Calories: 337; **Total Fat:** 12.9 g

Saturated Fat: 3.0 g; **Trans Fat:** 0 g

Protein: 41.7 g

Total Carbs: 11.8 g; **Net Carbs:** 9.9 g

Dietary Fiber: 1.9 g; **Sugars:** 8.9 g

Cholesterol: 102 mg; **Sodium:** 250 mg

Potassium: 600 mg; **Iron:** 23%

Vitamin A: 24%; **Vitamin C**: 83%; **Calcium**: 02%

Ingredients:

- [ ] 1 ½ pounds salmon, filet or steaks
- [ ] 3 tablespoons olive oil
- [ ] 1/2 teaspoon salt
- [ ] 1/4 teaspoon black pepper, ground

For the salsa:

- [ ] 2 teaspoons Splenda
- [ ] 2 teaspoons cider vinegar
- [ ] 1 teaspoon garlic, bottled, minced
- [ ] 1/4 teaspoon cumin, ground
- [ ] 1 red bell pepper, seeded, chopped
- [ ] 1/2 red onion, chopped

- ☐ 1 cup fresh pineapple, chopped into 1-inch cubes
- ☐ 2 medium tomatoes, chopped
- ☐ 1 fresh mango (100 g) peeled, seeded, chopped
- ☐ 1/2 cup fresh cilantro, chopped

Directions:
1. In mixing bowl, combine the vinegar, minced garlic, Splenda, and cumin until well combined and the sugar is dissolved.
2. Add in the bell pepper, onion, pineapple, tomatoes, mango, and the cilantro. Stir to combine. Set aside.
3. Heat a skillet over medium or medium-high heat.
4. Rub oil all over the salmon. Season with the salt and pepper. Put in the skillet and cook for about 3-4 minutes per side or until the fish is cooked through. Place the salmons on plates. Top with the mango-pineapple salsa.

Teriyaki Chicken

Prep Time: 05 minutes   **Cook Time:** 15 minutes

Serving Size: 188 g   **Serves:** 6

Calories: 299; **Total Fat:** 9.8 g

Saturated Fat: 0.6 g; **Trans Fat:** 0 g

Protein: 49.7 g

Total Carbs: 2.5 g; **Net Carbs:** 1.8 g

Dietary Fiber: 0.7 g; **Sugars:** 0.0 g

Cholesterol: 130 mg; **Sodium:** 689 mg

Potassium: 426 mg; **Iron:** 13%

Vitamin A: 0%; **Vitamin C:** 0%; **Calcium:** 03%

Ingredients:
- ☐ 1 tablespoon olive oil
- ☐ 1/2 teaspoon garlic powder
- ☐ 1/8 teaspoon black pepper, ground
- ☐ 2 pounds chicken breast, boneless, skinless
- ☐ 2 teaspoons sesame seeds, toasted

For the sauce:
- ☐ 3 tablespoons soy sauce, low-sodium
- ☐ 2 tablespoons Splenda (3 packets stevia)
- ☐ 1 tablespoon rice vinegar, seasoned
- ☐ 1/2 cup chicken broth or vegetable broth, reduced sodium
- ☐ 1 teaspoon cornstarch

☐ 2 teaspoons dark sesame oil

Directions:
1. Except for the sesame oil, whisk together the rest of the sauce ingredients. Add in the sesame oil. Whisk again. Set aside.
2. With a meat mallet, flatten the chicken breasts to ¼- inch thickness. Pat dry with a paper towel. Season with the pepper and the garlic powder.
3. Over medium-high heat, heat the skillet. Put the chicken and cook for about 3 minutes each side.
4. Pour the sauce into the skillet. Stir. Reduce the heat to low. Cook for about 3-4 minutes or until the sauce is thick and the chicken is cooked through.
5. Transfer the chicken into plates. Spoon the sauce over the meat. Sprinkle with sesame seeds. Serve.

Creamy Bacony Shrimp

Prep Time: 05 minutes   **Cook Time:** 15 minutes

Serving Size: 89 g   **Serves:** 4

Calories: 198; **Total Fat:** 16.2 g

Saturated Fat: 5.5; **Trans Fat:** 0 g

Protein: 12.1 g

Total Carbs: 1.5 g; **Net Carbs:** 1.5 g

Dietary Fiber: 0 g; **Sugars:** 0 g

Cholesterol: 90 mg; **Sodium:** 556 mg

Potassium: 174 mg; **Iron:** 05%

Vitamin A: 06%; **Vitamin C:** 01%; **Calcium:** 04%

Ingredients:

- ☐ 1/2 cup of smoked salmon, cut into strips
- ☐ 4 slices bacon, uncured, organic, cut into 1-inch pieces
- ☐ 4 ounces shrimp, raw, shelled
- ☐ 1 cup mushrooms, sliced
- ☐ 1/2 cup heavy whipping cream (use coconut cream for dairy-free option)
- ☐ 1 pinch sea salt
- ☐ Freshly ground black pepper
- ☐ 2 tablespoon olive oil

Directions:

1. Heat the skillet over medium heat. Heat the olive oil. Put the bacon in, cook until the bacon is done, but not crispy.
2. Add in the mushrooms. Cook for 5 minutes.
3. Add in the salmon. Cook for 2-3 minutes.
4. Add in the shrimp. Adjust heat to high. Sauté for 2 minutes.
5. Add in the cream and the salt. Lower the flame. Cook for 1 minute more, or until the cream is thick according to desired thickness. Serve immediately over zucchini or shirataki noodles.

Almond Cheesy Chicken

Prep Time: 10 minutes   **Cook Time:** 15 minutes

Serving Size: 217 g   **Serves**: 4

Calories: 432; **Total Fat:** 20.3 g

Saturated Fat: 6.1 g; **Trans Fat**: 0 g

Protein: 58.8 g

Total Carbs: 3.7 g; **Net Carbs:** 2.3 g

Dietary Fiber: 1.4 g; **Sugars:** 0.6 g

Cholesterol: 173 mg; **Sodium**: 640 mg

Potassium: 549 mg; **Iron:** 19%

Vitamin A: 11%; **Vitamin C**: 04%; **Calcium**: 07%

Ingredients:
- ☐ 4 chicken breasts (about 6 ounces each), boneless, skinless
- ☐ ½ cup of cream cheese
- ☐ 2 tablespoons chicken broth or vegetable broth, reduced sodium
- ☐ 1/4 teaspoon black pepper, ground
- ☐ 1/4 cup almonds, slivered and toasted, chopped
- ☐ 1/4 cup fresh chives, chopped
- ☐ 1/2 teaspoon salt
- ☐ 1 teaspoon olive oil
- ☐ 1 teaspoon butter
- ☐ 1 tablespoon fresh oregano, chopped

Directions:

1. In a small mixing bowl, combine the cream cheese, almonds, chives, and oregano together.
2. Slightly pound the chicken breasts to even the thickness of the meat. Pat dry with paper towel. At the top of each breast, using a small knife, carefully cut a pocket into the center for the filling, about 2/3 of the way down.
3. Fil each pocket with 1/4 of the cheese filling. Secure the opening with a toothpick.
4. Heat a large skillet over medium high heat. Season the outside of the chicken breasts with salt and pepper.
5. Put the oil and the butter into the skillet. Add in the chicken. Cook for about 5-6 minutes on each side or until cooked through and golden brown.
6. When cooked, remove the chicken from the skillet and transfer into a serving plate. Cover with foil to keep warm.
7. Pour the broth into the skillet to deglaze. Slice the chicken. Pour the sauce over the chicken. Serve.

Cheesy Spinach Chicken

Prep Time: 10 minutes	**Cook Time:** 15 minutes

Serving Size: 273 g   **Serves:** 4

Calories: 413; **Total Fat:** 17 g

Saturated Fat: 5.1 g; **Trans Fat:** 0 g

Protein: 61.9 g

Total Carbs: 2.4 g; **Net Carbs:** 1.6 g

Dietary Fiber: 0.8 g; **Sugars:** 0.0 g

Cholesterol: 168 mg; **Sodium:** 786 mg

Potassium: 671 mg; **Iron:** 19%

Vitamin A: 61%; **Vitamin C:** 15%; **Calcium:** 21%

Ingredients:

- ☐ 1 ½ pounds chicken breast (4 pieces), boneless, skinless
- ☐ 4 cups fresh baby spinach
- ☐ 3/4 cups mozzarella cheese, part-skim milk, low moisture, shredded
- ☐ 1 tablespoon olive oil
- ☐ 1/2 teaspoon garlic powder
- ☐ 1/2 teaspoon black pepper, ground
- ☐ 1/2 teaspoon salt
- ☐ 2 teaspoons garlic, bottled, minced
- ☐ 3/4 cup chicken broth or vegetable broth, reduced sodium

Directions:

1. Chop 2 cups of the spinach and then place them in a medium mixing bowl.
2. Add in the cheese and the garlic. Mix well.
3. Cut the side of the breast to open it like a butterfly. Divide the spinach-cheese mixture into four portions. Put a filling on the center of one side. Fold to close, and then secure with a toothpick. Season the outside with garlic powder, salt, and pepper.
4. Place a large skillet over medium or medium high heat. Pour the olive oil. Put the chicken in the skillet. Cook for about 2-3 minutes each side or until the meat is no longer pink. Remove the chicken and transfer to a large plate.
5. In the same skillet, put the remaining spinach. Pour in the broth. Cook for about 1 minute or until just wilted.
6. Divide the spinach between 4 plates. Place a chicken breast on top of each bed of spinach. Spoon the sauce over the chicken.

Lemony Chicken with Sautéed Baby Spinach

Prep Time: 10 minutes   **Cook Time:** 15 minutes

Serving Size: 280 g   **Serves:** 4

Calories: 416; **Total Fat:** 13.2 g

Saturated Fat: 2.5 g; **Trans Fat:** 0 g

Protein: 57.4 g

Total Carbs: 10.8 g; **Net Carbs:** 9.7 g

Dietary Fiber: 1.1 g; **Sugars:** 0.8 g

Cholesterol: 154 mg; **Sodium:** 338 mg

Potassium: 677 mg; **Iron:** 21%

Vitamin A: 58%; **Vitamin C:** 14%; **Calcium:** 06%

Ingredients:

- ☐ 4 cups baby spinach, fresh
- ☐ 1 ½ pounds chicken breast, boneless and skinless
- ☐ 1 tablespoon butter, light
- ☐ 1/3 cup coconut flour
- ☐ 1/2 teaspoon black pepper, ground
- ☐ 1/2 cups white dry wine
- ☐ 1/2 cups or vegetable broth chicken broth, reduced sodium
- ☐ 1 teaspoon Italian seasoning
- ☐ 1 teaspoon garlic salt
- ☐ 1 tablespoon olive oil

Directions:
1. For dredging, put the flour and the pepper into a baking pan or a plate. Mix well.
2. With a meat pallet, pound the chicken until slightly flattened.
3. Put the oil and the butter in a large skillet. Let the butter melt over medium heat. Dredge the chicken in the flour mixture. Shake off excess. Put the chicken into the skillet. Cook for about 3 minutes per side, or until browned lightly.
4. Pour in the broth into the skillet. Add in the wine, garlic salt, and the Italian seasoning. Continue cooking for about 5 minutes on medium-high heat, or until the sauce is reduced and thickened and the chicken is cooked thoroughly.
5. Remove the chicken and transfer to a plate.
6. In the same skillet, add in the spinach. Cook for about 1-2 minutes or until wilted. Pour the spinach sauce over the chicken. Serve.

Cheesy Turkey Pear Salad

Prep Time: 10 minutes   **Cook Time:** 15 minutes

Serving Size: 365 g   **Serves:** 4

Calories: 21.8; **Total Fat:** 6.6 g

Saturated Fat: 0.0 g; **Trans Fat:** 0 g

Protein: 36.3 g

Total Carbs: 8.8 g; **Net Carbs:** 7.2 g

Dietary Fiber: 1.6 g; **Sugars:** 5.1 g

Cholesterol: 64 mg; **Sodium:** 340 mg

Potassium: 215 mg; **Iron:** 12%

Vitamin A: 22%; **Vitamin C:** 11%; **Calcium:** 27%

Ingredients:

- ☐ 1 pound turkey tenderloin
- ☐ 8 cups arugula
- ☐ 4 slices provolone cheese, halved
- ☐ 2 tablespoons cider vinegar
- ☐ 2 pears, cored and sliced
- ☐ 1/4 cup olive oil
- ☐ 1 tablespoon honey mustard
- ☐ Salt and ground black pepper

Directions:

1. Cut the turkey crosswise into eight pieces 1-inch slices. With the palm of the hand, slightly flatten.

Season with salt and pepper. Brush the meat with 1/2 of the honey mustard.

2. In a 12-inch skillet, heat 2 tablespoons of the olive oil over medium-high heat. Put the turkey in the skillet in an even layer. Cook for about 2-3 minutes per side or until browned.

3. Layer the pears on top of the turkey. Top each pear with a half-slice of cheese. Reduce the heat to medium-low. Cover the skillet with the lid. Cook for about 3-4 minutes, or until the pear is warm and the cheese is melted.

4. Divide the arugula into 4 portions in serving dishes. Top with turkey slices.

5. For the sauce, whisk the remaining oil and honey mustard sauce, and the vinegar with the juices in the skillet. Cook for about 30 seconds. Drizzle the sauce over each serve. Sprinkle with additional pepper.

Lunch Keto Omelet

Prep Time: 15 minutes   **Cook Time:** 10 minutes

Serving Size: 364 g   **Serves:** 3

Calories: 718; **Total Fat:** 59.0 g

Saturated Fat: 27.5 g; **Trans Fat:** 0 g

Protein: 38.8 g

Total Carbs: 12.4 g; **Net Carbs:** 9 g

Dietary Fiber: 3.4 g; **Sugars:** 6.3 g

Cholesterol: 371 mg; **Sodium:** 297 mg

Potassium: 753 mg; **Iron:** 21%

Vitamin A: 17%; **Vitamin C:** 29%; **Calcium:** 22%

Ingredients:

- [ ] 6 eggs
- [ ] 1/2 cup cheddar cheese, grated
- [ ] 1 cup coconut milk
- [ ] 1/4 cup tomato, fresh
- [ ] 1/4 cup cabbage
- [ ] 1/4 cup broccoli florets
- [ ] 3 cloves garlic, finely chopped
- [ ] 1 large red onion, finely chopped
- [ ] 1 cup tuna (in water), drained, chopped coarsely
- [ ] Salt and pepper to taste
- [ ] 4 tablespoon olive oil

Directions:

1. Crack the eggs in a large mixing bowl. Add in the coconut milk and season with salt and pepper. Beat together. Set aside.
2. Grease a large skillet with cooking oil. When hot, add in the onion and the garlic. Sauté.
3. Add in the spinach, cabbage, tomato, tuna, and the broccoli. Cook, stirring, for about 2-3 minutes, until just cooked.
4. Pour the egg mixture over the vegetables. Cook undisturbed for about 4 minutes, or until the eggs are set. When firm, cut into 4 wedges. Flip over each wedge. When cooked, garnish with cheese. Enjoy.

Pesto, Pine Nuts and Cheese Stuffed Chicken

Prep Time: 10 minutes   **Cook Time:** 20 minutes

Serving Size: 202 g **Serves:** 4	

Serving Size: 202 g   **Serves:** 4

Calories: 374; **Total Fat:** 17.7 g

Saturated Fat: 4.3 g; **Trans Fat:** 0 g

Protein: 51.2 g

Total Carbs: 2 g; **Net Carbs:** 1.4 g

Dietary Fiber: 0.6 g; **Sugars:** 0.9 g

Cholesterol: 138 mg; **Sodium:** 570 mg

Potassium: 429 mg; **Iron:** 13%

Vitamin A: 05%; **Vitamin C:** 00%; **Calcium:** 15%

Ingredients:
- ☐ 1 ¼ pounds chicken breast (4 pieces), boneless, skinless
- ☐ 1/2 cup mozzarella cheese, part skim milk, low moisture, shredded, divided into 4 portions
- ☐ 1/2 cup chicken broth or vegetable broth, reduced sodium
- ☐ 1/4 teaspoon black pepper, ground
- ☐ 1/4 teaspoon salt
- ☐ 2 tablespoons pine nuts, toasted, divided into 4 portions
- ☐ 2 tablespoons pesto sauce (prepared), divided into 4 portions
- ☐ 2 teaspoons olive oil

☐ Fresh basil, chopped

Directions:

1. In a lengthwise manner, cut the chicken breast to open it like a book or butterfly.
2. Spread the pesto on one side of the inside of the chicken. Add the cheese and the pine nuts. Fold the chicken to close. Secure with toothpicks. Season the chicken with salt and pepper.
3. Place a large skillet over medium-high heat. Pour oil into the skillet. Put in the chicken. Cook for about 5 minutes per side.
4. Pour in the chicken broth, deglazing the pan. Lower the heat. Bring to simmer. Place the lid on the skillet. Turn the heat off. Let sit for 2-3 minutes. Transfer each chicken breast on to separate plates. Spoon broth over each serving. Top each with fresh basil.

Hamburger Cabbage Stir-Fry

Prep Time: 10 minutes	**Cook Time:** 20 minutes

Serving Size: 202 g   **Serves:** 6
Calories: 234; **Total Fat:** 9.1 g
Saturated Fat: 2.4 g; **Trans Fat:** 0 g
Protein: 25.6 g
Total Carbs: 11.7 g; **Net Carbs:** 10 g
Dietary Fiber: 1.7 g; **Sugars:** 0.8 g
Cholesterol: 74 mg; **Sodium:** 371s mg
Potassium: 590 mg; **Iron:** 89%
Vitamin A: 07%; **Vitamin C:** 45%; **Calcium:** 04%

Ingredients:

- ☐ 1 ¾ cups coleslaw mix
- ☐ 2 ½ cup fresh mushrooms, sliced
- ☐ 2 teaspoons granular Splenda, optional
- ☐ 2 tablespoons soy sauce
- ☐ 2 cloves garlic, minced
- ☐ 6 tablespoons sesame oil
- ☐ 1/4 pound beef, ground
- ☐ 1 bunch (3 ounces after trimming) green onions (about 8 onions), cut on the bias
- ☐ Salt and pepper, to taste

Optional:

- ☐ Pinch of ginger
- ☐ Pinch of cayenne

Directions:
1. In a very large skillet, brown the ground beef and garlic, seasoning with little salt and pepper. Drain the excess fat.
2. Add in the cabbage and the mushrooms. Fry, stirring constantly, until the cabbage is tender-crisp.
3. Add the remaining ingredients. Continue cooking until heated through. Adjust seasoning to your preference

Gooey Sausage Pops

Prep Time: 10 minutes   **Cook Time:** 20 minutes

Serving Size: 74 g **Serves:** 10	
Calories: 196; **Total Fat:** 15.4 g	
Saturated Fat: 5.6 g; **Trans Fat:** 0.1 g	
Protein: 12.5 g	
Total Carbs: 1.2 g; **Net Carbs:** 1.2 g	
Dietary Fiber: 0 g; **Sugars:** 0.5 g	
Cholesterol: 61 mg; **Sodium:** 428 mg	
Potassium: 181 mg; **Iron:** 05%	
Vitamin A: 04%; **Vitamin C:** 19%; **Calcium:** 06%	

Ingredients:

- ☐ 2 cups sausages, shredded
- ☐ 1/4 teaspoon mustard powder
- ☐ 1/2 cup red peppers
- ☐ 1/2 cup cottage cheese
- ☐ 1/2 cup cheddar cheese
- ☐ 1 teaspoon chili flakes
- ☐ 1 egg

Directions:

1. Except for the eggs, combine the rest of the ingredients together. Shape into balls.
2. Crack the eggs into a bowl. Dip each ball in the egg. Fry in a deep skillet until golden color and crusty.

Dinner

Tuscan Pork Chops

Prep Time: 05 minutes   **Cook Time:** 15 minutes

Serving Size: 134 g **Serves:** 4	
Calories: 254; **Total Fat:** 20.4 g	
Saturated Fat: 6.0 g; **Trans Fat:** 0 g	
Protein: 12.9 g	
Total Carbs: 5.3 g; **Net Carbs:** 3.9 g	
Dietary Fiber: 1.4 g; **Sugars:** 2.3 g	
Cholesterol: 46 mg; **Sodium:** 41 mg	
Potassium: 347 mg; **Iron:** 05%	
Vitamin A: 09%; **Vitamin C:** 16%; **Calcium:** 04%	

Ingredients:

- ☐ 4 pork chops
- ☐ 1 ½ cups fresh tomatoes, diced
- ☐ 5 cloves garlic, diced
- ☐ 2 teaspoon oregano
- ☐ 1 teaspoon sage
- ☐ 1 teaspoon basil
- ☐ 3 tablespoons olive oil
- ☐ 1 large onion, diced

Directions:

1. Heat a large cast iron skillet over high heat until warm.
2. Pour in the oil and heat for about 20 seconds, or until simmering, but not smoking or burning.
3. Brown the pork chops for about 1 minute on each side.
4. Reduce the heat to medium-low. Add in the onions. Stir the onions. Flip the pork chops after 2 minutes per side.
5. Add in the tomatoes, garlic, and other spices.
6. Simmer for about 5-8 minutes or until the tomatoes are soft and set.
7. Serve on a bed of pasta or zucchini noodles.

Skillet Steaks with Gorgonzola Cheesy Herbed Butter

Prep Time: 15 minutes	**Cook Time:** 10 minutes

Serving Size: 287 g **Serves**: 4
Calories: 950; **Total Fat:** 75 g
Saturated Fat: 30 g; **Trans Fat:** 0 g
Protein: 61 g
Total Carbs: 2 g; **Net Carbs:** <2 g
Dietary Fiber: <1 g; **Sugars:** 0 g
Cholesterol: 225 mg; **Sodium**: 560 mg
Potassium: 880 mg; **Iron**: 45%
Vitamin A: 10%; **Vitamin C**: 04%; **Calcium**: 08%

Ingredients:
For the steaks:
- ☐ 4 ribeye steaks, or your preferred cut
- ☐ Olive oil
- ☐ Salt
- ☐ Freshly ground black pepper

For the herbed butter:
- ☐ 4 tablespoons Gorgonzola cheese
- ☐ 4 tablespoons butter, softened
- ☐ 1 tablespoons fresh parsley, chopped

Directions:
1. With the salt and the pepper, season both sides of the steaks. Individually wrap each steak tightly

with a plastic wrap; marinate in the refrigerator for 4 hours or overnight. When ready to cook, remove from the refrigerator and let sit for about 30 minutes or until room temperature.

2. Over medium heat, heat a heavy, large cast-iron skillet until a drop of water dances in the bottom of the skillet when tested.

3. Coat the skillet well with the olive oil. Place the steaks in the skillet, cover, and cook for 2 minutes or until your preferred doneness.

4. Remove the skillet from the heat, let the steak rest inside for about 5 minutes.

5. Meanwhile, combine the butter, cheese, and parsley until creamy.

6. Serve the steaks with 1 tablespoon of the creamy butter mixture, allowing the mixture to melt over the sides.

Steak with Horseradish Cream Sauce

Prep Time: 05 minutes   **Cook Time:** 15 minutes

Serving Size: 209 g   **Serves:** 4

Calories: 413; **Total Fat:** 14.9 g

Saturated Fat: 5.8 g; **Trans Fat:** 0 g

Protein: 62.2 g

Total Carbs: 3.6 g; **Net Carbs:** 3.6 g

Dietary Fiber: 0 g; **Sugars:** 2.1 g

Cholesterol: 162 mg; **Sodium:** 484 mg

Potassium: 623 mg; **Iron:** 32%

Vitamin A: 03%; **Vitamin C:** 04%; **Calcium:** 05%

Ingredients:

- [ ] 1 ½ pounds steak, lean rib eye, boneless, fat trimmed
- [ ] 1 tablespoon fresh chives, chopped
- [ ] 1 teaspoon garlic, jarred, crushed
- [ ] 1/2 teaspoon black pepper, ground
- [ ] 1/2 teaspoon salt
- [ ] 1/3 cup sour cream, light or low fat
- [ ] 2 tablespoons horseradish, prepared
- [ ] 2 tablespoons Worcestershire sauce, low sodium
- [ ] 2 teaspoons olive oil

Directions:

1. In a small mixing bowl, mix the horseradish, cream, garlic, and chives. Set aside.
2. Season the steaks with salt, pepper, and the Worcestershire sauce.
3. Heat the skillet over medium high heat. Drizzle the olive oil over the steaks. Place on the skillet. Cook for about 5 minutes each side or until desired doneness.
4. Remove the steak from the skillet. Transfer to a plate. Cover with foil. Let the steak rest for about 5 minutes. Serve topped with the horseradish sauce, or serve the sauce on the side.

Salmon and Eggplant Curry

Prep Time: 10 minutes   **Cook Time:** 15 minutes

Serving Size: 268 g   **Serves:** 6

Calories: 394; **Total Fat:** 32.2 g

Saturated Fat: 24.6 g; **Trans Fat:** 0 g

Protein: 18.1 g

Total Carbs: 12.8 g; **Net Carbs:** 7.5 g

Dietary Fiber: 5.3 g; **Sugars:** 7.2 g

Cholesterol: 33 mg; **Sodium:** 396 mg

Potassium: 739 mg; **Iron:** 15%

Vitamin A: 08%; **Vitamin C:** 34%; **Calcium:** 07%

Ingredients:

- 1 pound salmon, fillet, skinned, cut into 1-inch pieces
- 1 medium eggplant (about 1 pound), cut into 1/2-inch cubes
- 2 cups sugar snap peas, trimmed
- 1 can (14-ounces) coconut milk
- 1 ½ tablespoon curry yellow Thai curry powder or normal curry powder
- 1 ½ tablespoon fish sauce
- 5 tablespoons coconut oil
- 1 tablespoon light brown sugar
- 1/2 cup fresh basil, chopped
- 2 cloves garlic, minced
- 3 tablespoons lime juice

Directions:
1. In a large skillet, heat the canola oil over medium heat.
2. Add in the curry powder and the garlic. Cook for about 1 minute, stirring, until fragrant. Add in the eggplant. Cook for about 2 minutes, stirring, until the eggplant is coated with the curry mixture.
3. Pour in the coconut milk, brown sugar, and fish sauce. Bring to a boil. Stir in the salmon and the snow peas. Reduce the heat to a simmer. Cook covered for about 5 minutes, occasionally stirring, until the fish is cooked through and the peas are tender-crisp. Remove from the heat. Stir in the lime juice and the basil. Serve with cauliflower rice.

Beef Tenderloin with Mushroom Sauce

Prep Time: 05 minutes   **Cook Time:** 20 minutes

Serving Size: 355 g   **Serves:** 4

Calories: 413; **Total Fat:** 18.1 g

Saturated Fat: 7.5 g; **Trans Fat:** 0 g

Protein: 53.3 g

Total Carbs: 6.1 g; **Net Carbs:** 5.2 g

Dietary Fiber: 0.9 g; **Sugars:** 2.2 g

Cholesterol: 162 mg; **Sodium:** 412 mg

Potassium: 1173 mg; **Iron:** 23%

Vitamin A: 01%; **Vitamin C:** 01%; **Calcium:** 06%

Ingredients:

- [ ] 4 pieces (6 ounces each) beef tenderloin, lean
- [ ] 3/4 cup beef broth or vegetable broth, low sodium
- [ ] 2 teaspoons extra virgin olive oil,
- [ ] 2 teaspoons coconut flour
- [ ] 2 teaspoons light butter
- [ ] 1/4 teaspoon salt
- [ ] 1/2 teaspoon black pepper, ground
- [ ] 1/2 teaspoon garlic powder
- [ ] 1 tablespoon garlic, minced
- [ ] 1 pound Cremini or button or combination mushrooms, cleaned, sliced

Directions:

1. Season both sides of the meat with garlic powder, salt, and pepper. Allow to sit for about 5 minutes at room temperature.
2. In a large skillet, put in the butter and the olive oil. Heat over medium or medium-high heat.
3. Put in the meat. Sear for about 3-4 minutes each side or until your desired doneness. Transfer to a plate. Cover with a foil.
4. In the same skillet, put the mushrooms. Cook for about 2-3 minutes over medium-high heat until browned. Stir and cook for 2 minutes more.
5. Add in the garlic. Cook for 1 minute. Stir in the flour. Slowly pour the beef stock and stir well. Bring to a boil. Reduce heat and simmer until the sauce thickens. Pour over the tenderloin. Serve.

Chicken with Creamy Dijon Sauce

Prep Time: 05 minutes   **Cook Time:** 20 minutes

Serving Size: 165 g   **Serves:** 4

Calories: 241; **Total Fat:** 9.6 g

Saturated Fat: 3.5 g; **Trans Fat**: 0 g

Protein: 34.4 g

Total Carbs: 2.8 g; **Net Carbs:** 2.8 g

Dietary Fiber: 0 g; **Sugars:** 0 g

Cholesterol: 99 mg; **Sodium**: 344 mg

Potassium: 286 mg; **Iron:** 07%

Vitamin A: 03%; **Vitamin C**: 01%; **Calcium**: 05%

Ingredients:

- 1 pounds chicken breast, boneless, skinless
- 1 shallot, chopped
- 1 teaspoon garlic powder
- 1/2 cup half and half, fat free
- 1/4 teaspoon black pepper, grounded
- 1/4 teaspoon salt
- 2 tablespoons chicken broth or vegetable broth, reduced sodium
- 2 tablespoons Dijon mustard
- 2 teaspoons olive oil

Directions:

1. Pound the chicken breast to an even 1/4-inch thickness. Season with the garlic powder, salt, and pepper.
2. Heat a large skillet over medium-high heat. Add the oil into the skillet. Put the chicken. Cook for about 3-4 minutes each side. Reduce the heat. Cook the chicken until the meat is no longer pink. Remove the skillet from the heat.
3. Remove the chicken and transfer into a serving plate. Cover with foil to keep warm.
4. Return the skillet over medium-low heat. Put in the shallots. Cook for about 1-2 minutes, stirring occasionally.
5. Pour in the chicken broth. Simmer for about 2-3 minutes. Add in the half and half and the Dijon. Cook for about 1-2 minutes. Pour the sauce over the chicken.

Chicken with Pesto Sauce

Prep Time: 05 minutes   **Cook Time:** 20 minutes

Serving Size: 139 g   **Serves:** 4

Calories: 265; **Total Fat:** 12.7 g

Saturated Fat: 2.9 g; **Trans Fat:** 0 g

Protein: 34.4 g

Total Carbs: 1.8 g; **Net Carbs:** 1.8 g

Dietary Fiber: 0 g; **Sugars:** 0.9 g

Cholesterol: 93 mg; **Sodium:** 437 mg

Potassium: 235 mg; **Iron:** 07%

Vitamin A: 03%; **Vitamin C:** 01%; **Calcium:** 06%

Ingredients:

- ☐ 1 ½ pounds chicken breast, boneless, skinless
- ☐ 3 tablespoons pesto sauce
- ☐ 1 tablespoon fresh basil, chopped
- ☐ 1 tablespoon olive oil
- ☐ 1 teaspoon garlic powder
- ☐ 1/2 teaspoon black pepper, ground
- ☐ 1/2 teaspoon salt
- ☐ 2 tablespoons half and half, fat free

Directions:

1. Cut the chicken breasts into 4 portions. Pound the breasts into 1/2-inch thickness. Season with the garlic powder, salt, and pepper.
2. Heat a large skillet over medium-high heat. Pour in the olive oil. In a single layer, add the chicken.

Cook for about 3-4 minutes per side, or until cooked through and golden brown. Transfer the chicken into a plate. Cover with foil.

3. In the same skillet, pour the half and half and the pesto into the skillet. Adjust heat to low. Stir and cook until warm. Spoon the sauce over the chicken. Serve. Garnish with basil, if desired.

Pesto Chicken with Relish

Prep Time: 10 minutes   **Cook Time:** 15 minutes

Serving Size: 197 g   **Serves:** 4

Calories: 357; **Total Fat:** 19.3 g

Saturated Fat: 5 g; **Trans Fat**: 0 g

Protein: 41.6 g

Total Carbs: 4.6 g; **Net Carbs:** 2.4 g

Dietary Fiber: 2.2 g; **Sugars:** 1.5 g

Cholesterol: 114 mg; **Sodium:** 560 mg

Potassium: 506 mg; **Iron:** 11%

Vitamin A: 10%; **Vitamin C**: 12%; **Calcium:** 15%

Ingredients:

- 1 pound chicken breast, boneless, skinless
- 1 tablespoon fresh basil, chopped
- 1/2 avocado, peeled, chopped
- 1/2 teaspoon salt
- 1/4 teaspoon black pepper, ground
- 2 ounces mozzarella cheese, part skim milk, low-moisture, sliced
- 2 tablespoons pesto sauce
- 2 teaspoons garlic, bottled, minced
- 2 teaspoons olive oil
- 2 medium tomatoes, chopped

Directions:

1. In a mixing bowl, combine the tomatoes, avocado, garlic, and basil until well incorporated. Set aside.
2. From the thickest chicken end, carefully cut a slit down the side, making sure not to cut all the way through, and opening it like a butterfly or book.
3. Spread the pesto sauce on one side of the chicken (on the inside of part). Place 1 slice of cheese on top of the pesto. Fold close and secure with a toothpick.
4. Season the outside with salt and pepper.
5. Preheat the oven to 400F.
6. Place a large oven-safe skillet over medium-high heat. Put in the oil. Put the chicken into the skillet. Cook for about 5 minutes per side.
7. Transfer the skillet into the oven. Bake for about 5 minutes or until the chicken is cooked through.
8. Transfer the chicken into a serving plate. Top with the tomato-avocado relish.

Chicken Pomodoro

Prep Time: 10 minutes   **Cook Time:** 20 minutes

Serving Size: 298 g   **Serves**: 4

Calories: 328; **Total Fat:** 2.8 g

Saturated Fat: 0 g; **Trans Fat**: 0 g

Protein: 48.3 g

Total Carbs: 5.7 g; **Net Carbs:** 4.6 g

Dietary Fiber: 1.1 g; **Sugars:** 2.1 g

Cholesterol: 133 mg; **Sodium**: 614 mg

Potassium: 623 mg; **Iron**: 13%

Vitamin A: 16%; **Vitamin C**: 21%; **Calcium**: 07%

Ingredients:

- ☐ 1 ¼ pounds chicken breast, boneless, skinless
- ☐ 4 Roma tomatoes
- ☐ 3/4 cup chicken broth or vegetable broth, reduced sodium
- ☐ 1 tablespoon lemon juice
- ☐ 1 tablespoon olive oil
- ☐ 1/2 cup half and half, fat free
- ☐ 1/2 teaspoon cornstarch
- ☐ 1/2 teaspoon black pepper, ground
- ☐ 1/2 teaspoon salt
- ☐ 2 green onions, chopped
- ☐ 2 teaspoons garlic, bottled, minced
- ☐ 1/4 cup fresh basil, chopped

Directions:
1. Cut the chicken in half. Pound to an even 1/4-inch thickness. Season with salt and pepper, and if desired, with a little paprika.
2. In a large skillet, heat olive oil over medium high heat. Put the chicken. Cook for about 3-4 minutes each side or until cooked through and browned. Remove and transfer to a plate.
3. Adjust the heat to medium. In the same skillet, add in the garlic. Cook, stirring for about 30 seconds. Add the chopped tomatoes. Cook, stirring for about 1 minute.
4. Pour in the broth and the lemon juice. Stir and cook for about 5 minutes over medium heat. Stir in the green onions. Mix in the cornstarch and the half and half in a small cup. Pour into the skillet.
5. Return the chicken to the skillet. Continue cooking for about 3 minutes more, or until the sauce thickens. Serve the chicken with the sauce poured over. Garnish with the basil.

Chicken Georgia

Prep Time: 05 minutes   **Cook Time:** 30 minutes

Serving Size: 260 g **Serves**: 4	
Calories: 150; **Total Fat:** 13 g	
Saturated Fat: 8 g; **Trans Fat**: 0 g	
Protein: 4 g	
Total Carbs: 4 g; **Net Carbs:** 8.5 g	
Dietary Fiber: 1.0 g; **Sugars:** 2.0 g	
Cholesterol: 35 mg; **Sodium**: 28 mg	
Potassium: 230 mg; **Iron**: 04%	
Vitamin A: 08%; **Vitamin C**: 06%; **Calcium**: 06%	

Ingredients:
- [ ] 4 tablespoons butter (1/2 stick) or ghee
- [ ] 4 skinless boneless (about 6-8 ounce each) chicken breast halves (use very small breasts or large fillet, cut thick ones into halves)
- [ ] 8 ounce fresh mushrooms, sliced
- [ ] 1 small onion chopped
- [ ] 1 cup mozzarella, shredded

For the chicken seasoning:
- [ ] 3/4-1 tsp of salt
- [ ] 1/2 tsp garlic powder
- [ ] 1/4 tsp pepper

For the mushroom mixture:

93

☐ 1/4 tsp salt

☐ 1/4 tsp pepper

Directions:

1. Season the all the sides of the chicken breasts with the chicken seasoning.
2. Melt the butter or ghee in a large-sized skillet. Add the onions and mushrooms, sprinkle with the salt and pepper for the mushroom; cook for about 10 minutes, stirring occasionally, until tender.
3. Add the chicken nestling it between the mushrooms so the meat makes contact with the skillet; cook for about 7 to 10 per side, or until cooked through, stirring the mushrooms occasionally.
4. When the chicken is cooked, remove from the pan and transfer into a serving platter. Sprinkle the cheese over the still hot chicken meat, and place the mushroom mixtures on top; let sit for a couple of minutes until the cheese melts.

To serve from the pan:

1. Once the chicken is cooked, but still in the pan; sprinkle with the cheese, turn the heat off, and let the cheese melt.

Notes:

You can use smoked cheese, too. To cook the chicken quicker, loosely tent the skillet. This will make the skillet saucier, too.

Curried Fish

Prep Time: 15 minutes	**Cook Time:** 20 minutes

Serving Size: 224 g   **Serves**: 6

Calories: 470; **Total Fat:** 37.4 g

Saturated Fat: 27.4 g; **Trans Fat**: 0 g

Protein: 27.5 g

Total Carbs: 8.9 g; **Net Carbs:** 5.6 g

Dietary Fiber: 3.3 g; **Sugars:** 4.1 g

Cholesterol: 29 mg; **Sodium**: 28449 mg

Potassium: 618 mg; **Iron:** 16%

Vitamin A: 17%; **Vitamin C**: 51%; **Calcium**: 04%

Ingredients:

- ☐ 1 can (14-ounce) coconut milk
- ☐ 1 green bell pepper, diced
- ☐ 1 onion, finely chopped
- ☐ 1 teaspoon fresh thyme, chopped
- ☐ 1 teaspoon minced chili pepper, or to taste
- ☐ 1 teaspoon salt
- ☐ 2 cloves garlic, minced
- ☐ 1 ¼ pounds mahi-mahi fillets, skinned, cut into 1-inch pieces
- ☐ 2 tablespoons curry powder
- ☐ 3 scallions, thinly sliced
- ☐ 6 tablespoons coconut oil

Serve with:

Cauliflower rice

Directions:
1. In a large skillet, heat the oil over medium heat.
2. Add in the curry powder and cook for about 1 minute.
3. Add the onion, garlic, bell pepper, and thyme. Cook, stirring, for about 2 minutes, or until fragrant.
4. Pour in the coconut milk. Bring to simmer. Stir in the fish and the scallion. Cook covered for about 5-7 minutes until the fish is cooked through.
5. Stir in the salt. Serve immediately.

Steaks, Horseradish, and Slaw

Prep Time: 20 minutes   **Cook Time:** 20 minutes

Serving Size: 264 g   **Serves:** 4

Calories: 334; **Total Fat:** 12.4 g

Saturated Fat: 3.2 g; **Trans Fat:** 0 g

Protein: 42.8 g

Total Carbs: 11.4 g; **Net Carbs:** 8.8 g

Dietary Fiber: 2.6 g; **Sugars:** 6.6 g

Cholesterol: 103 mg; **Sodium:** 592 mg

Potassium: 766 mg; **Iron:** 31%

Vitamin A: 95%; **Vitamin C:** 22%; **Calcium:** 08%

Ingredients:

- ☐ 1 pound (1-1 ¼ inch thick) strip steak, trimmed, cut into 4 portions
- ☐ 1 tablespoon extra-virgin olive oil
- ☐ 1/4 cup white or regular balsamic vinegar
- ☐ 1/4 teaspoon freshly ground pepper
- ☐ 2 teaspoons extra-virgin olive oil
- ☐ 2 tablespoons dill, divided
- ☐ 3/4 teaspoon kosher salt

For the sauce:

- ☐ 2-4 tablespoons horseradish
- ☐ 1 tablespoon reduced-fat sour cream
- ☐ 1/4 cup water

☐ 1 tablespoons dill

For the vegetable slaw:
☐ 1 medium turnip (about 1 cup), peeled, shredded
☐ 1 cup beet, peeled, shredded
☐ 1 cup carrots, peeled, shredded
☐ 2 teaspoons extra-virgin olive oil
☐ 2 tablespoons dill
☐ 1/2 teaspoon kosher salt

Directions:
1. Toss the vegetable slaw ingredients together. Set aside.
2. Season the steak with the remaining 1/4 teaspoon salt and the pepper.
3. In a large skillet, heat the remaining 1 tablespoon oil over medium-high heat. When oil is heated, put the steaks in the skillet. Cook for about 3-5 minutes per side for medium-rare doneness, turning once and adjusting heat when necessary to prevent burning.
4. Remove the pan from the heat. Transfer the steaks into a plate to rest.
5. In the same skillet, pour in the water and the vinegar. Add in the horseradish. Scrape any brown bits and stir any accumulated juice left by the steaks.
6. Drizzle 1/2 of the sauce (about 1/4 cup) over the vegetable slaw. Toss to coat.

7. Into the remaining sauce in the skillet, stir in the sour cream and the remaining 1 tablespoon dill.
8. Divide the steak and the slaw into four plates. Drizzle with the sauce. Serve.

Asian-Style Pork Chops

Prep Time: 30 minutes   **Cook Time:** 20 minutes

Serving Size: 120 g   **Serves:** 4

Calories: 391; **Total Fat:** 4.3 g

Saturated Fat: 8 g; **Trans Fat:** 0 g

Protein: 4 g

Total Carbs: 4 g; **Net Carbs:** 4.3 g

Dietary Fiber: 0 g; **Sugars:** 2.6 g

Cholesterol: 69 mg; **Sodium:** 310 mg

Potassium: 331 mg; **Iron:** 06%

Vitamin A: 02%; **Vitamin C:** 08%; **Calcium:** 03%

Ingredients:

- 4 pork chops
- 3 scallions, chopped
- 1/2 teaspoon powdered ginger
- 1/2 tablespoon lime juice
- 1/2 tablespoon honey
- 4 tablespoon coconut oil
- 1 tablespoon coconut aminos
- 1 large garlic clove, minced

Directions:

1. In a large mixing bowl, combine the coconut aminos, coconut oil, lime juice, garlic, and ginger.

2. Put the pork chops in the bowl. Seal the bowl with a plastic wrap. Chill for about 25 minutes in the refrigerator.
3. Grease a skillet. Place over medium heat. Cook the pork chops until the meat is cooked through.
4. Transfer the pork chops into a serving dish. Sprinkle with scallions.

Seared Swordfish with Poached Tomatoes

Prep Time: 15 minutes   **Cook Time:** 50 minutes

Serving Size: 239 g   **Serves:** 4

Calories: 324; **Total Fat:** 32 g

Saturated Fat: 5 g; **Trans Fat:** 0 g

Protein: 24 g

Total Carbs: 5 g; **Net Carbs:** 3 g

Dietary Fiber: 2.0 g; **Sugars:** 2.0 g

Cholesterol: 45 mg; **Sodium:** 1490 mg

Potassium: 550 mg; **Iron:** 10%

Vitamin A: 20%; **Vitamin C:** 20%; **Calcium:** 04%

Ingredients:
- 1 pound swordfish, cut into 4 fillets
- 1 sprig fresh basil
- 1 sprig fresh mint
- 1 teaspoon hot sauce (Tabasco)
- 1/2 cup olive oil
- 2 cups cherry tomatoes
- 2 teaspoons salt
- Salt and pepper, to taste

Directions:
1. Preheat the oven to 425F.
2. In a heavy-bottomed, large oven-safe skillet, heat the oil. Add the tomatoes, stir to coat, then reduce the flame or heat to medium-low; cook, stirring occasionally, for 15 minutes. Add the hot sauce and

the pepper, stir to mix, and cover partially; continue cooking for 15 minutes more, until the tomato skin is shriveled and the blistered. With a slotted spoon, transfer the tomatoes into a clean plate.

3. In the same skillet, add the basil and the mint; stir around in the skillet for 1 minute, then discard them. Adjust the heat to medium-high.

4. Generously sprinkle both sides of the swordfish with the salt and pepper. Add the fillets into the pan; sear for 3 to 4 minutes, or until the bottom has a nice golden crust. Flip the fish in the skillet, transfer to the oven, and bake for 10 minutes.

5. Carefully remove the skillet from the oven. Transfer the fish into a serving platter, top with the poached tomatoes with the juices. Sprinkle with fresh herbs, if desired. Serve immediately.

Lamb Chops with Mint Chimichurri

Prep Time: 30 minutes   **Cook Time:** 30 minutes

Serving Size: 371 g   **Serves:** 4

Calories: 822; **Total Fat:** 52.6 g

Saturated Fat: 15 g; **Trans Fat:** 0 g

Protein: 80.8 g

Total Carbs: 4.1 g; **Net Carbs:** 2.7 g

Dietary Fiber: 1.4 g; **Sugars:** 0 g

Cholesterol: 272 mg; **Sodium:** 332 mg

Potassium: 1134 mg; **Iron:** 51%

Vitamin A: 41%; **Vitamin C:** 38%; **Calcium:** 09%

Ingredients:
For the grilled lamb chops:
- [ ] 16 lamb rib chops, frenched
- [ ] 2 tablespoons ghee or oil of choice, melted
- [ ] Freshly ground black pepper
- [ ] Kosher salt

For the mint chimichurri:
- [ ] 1 tablespoon capers, salt-packed, soaked, rinsed, drained, and minced
- [ ] 1/4 teaspoon red chili flakes, crushed
- [ ] 1/4 cup minced shallots
- [ ] 1/4 cup balsamic vinegar
- [ ] 1/2 cup fresh mint, chopped

- [ ] 1/2 cup extra-virgin olive oil
- [ ] 1 teaspoon garlic cloves, minced
- [ ] 1 cup fresh parsley, chopped
- [ ] freshly ground black pepper

Directions:

1. Salt both sides of a lamb chops. Bring them to a room temperature on the counter.
2. Meanwhile, make the chimichurri. Except for the olive oil, put the rest of the chimichurri ingredients in a blender. Pulse until the contents are roughly chopped. Resume pulsing while slowly adding the olive oil in a steady stream. When the mixture is smooth, pour into deep, large dish that can hold all of the lamb chops.
3. Pat dry the lamb chops with a paper towel. Season with the pepper. Brush with the melted ghee.
4. Heat cast-iron skillet over medium heat. Cook the chops for about 2-3 minutes per side or until the meat is cooked to desired doneness.
5. When cooked to desired doneness, put the chops into the chimichurri. Toss to coat well. Let rest for 10 minutes. Serve.

Snacks
Garlicky Sesame Bok Choy

Prep Time: 05 minutes   **Cook Time:** 05 minutes

Serving Size: 119 g   **Serves:** 4

Calories: 61; **Total Fat:** 5.3 g

Saturated Fat: 0.8 g; **Trans Fat:** 0 g

Protein: 1.7 g

Total Carbs: 2.7 g; **Net Carbs:** 1.6 g

Dietary Fiber: 1.1 g; **Sugars:** 1.4 g

Cholesterol: 0 mg; **Sodium:** 74 mg

Potassium: 289 mg; **Iron:** 05%

Vitamin A: 101%; **Vitamin C:** 85%; **Calcium:** 12%

Ingredients:
- ☐ 1 pound baby bok choy, sliced lengthwise into halves or quarters, rinse, pat dry
- ☐ 1 teaspoon garlic, bottled minced
- ☐ 1 ½ tablespoons sesame oil, dark

Directions:
1. Over medium heat, heat a large skillet.
2. Heat a large skillet over medium heat. Add sesame oil and the garlic and stir.
3. Add the bok choy and stir fry for about 2 minutes until tender-crisp.
4. Remove from the skillet and serve on a plate.
5. Season with salt and pepper or a little low sodium soy sauce if desired.

Asparagus with Asian Dip

Prep Time: 05 minutes   **Cook Time:** 05 minutes

Serving Size: 191 g   **Serves:** 4

Calories: 463; **Total Fat:** 46 g

Saturated Fat: 17.9 g; **Trans Fat:** 0 g

Protein: 3.4 g

Total Carbs: 13.8 g; **Net Carbs:** 11.2 g

Dietary Fiber: 2.6 g; **Sugars:** 3.4 g

Cholesterol: 66 mg; **Sodium:** 455 mg

Potassium: 267 mg; **Iron:** 15%

Vitamin A: 32%; **Vitamin C:** 13%; **Calcium:** 05%

Ingredients:
- 1 pound asparagus, fresh
- 1/2 cup butter
- 4 tablespoons olive oil
- 1/2 teaspoon ground black pepper
- 6 garlic cloves, minced

For the sauce:
- 1 teaspoon rice vinegar, seasoned
- 1/3 cup mayonnaise, reduced fat or light
- 2 teaspoons honey or agave nectar
- 2 teaspoons dark sesame oil, or more if desired
- 2 teaspoons soy sauce, low sodium

Directions:

1. In a skillet over medium high heat, melt the butter
2. Put in the olive oil, salt, and pepper.
3. Add in the garlic. Cook for about 1 minute, but not browned.
4. Put in the asparagus. Cook for about 10 minutes, turning the spears to cook evenly. Place on serving platter.
5. In a small bowl, mix all of the sauce ingredients together. Chill until ready to serve. Serve beside the platter of asparagus.

Bok Choy Stir Fry with Cashews

Prep Time: 05 minutes   **Cook Time:** 05 minutes

Serving Size: 161 g   **Serves:** 4

Calories: 151; **Total Fat:** 12.7 g

Saturated Fat: 2.0 g; **Trans Fat**: 0 g

Protein: 3.5 g

Total Carbs: 8 g; **Net Carbs:** 10 g

Dietary Fiber: 2.0 g; **Sugars:** 3.0 g

Cholesterol: 0 mg; **Sodium:** 226 mg

Potassium: 380 mg; **Iron**: 09%

Vitamin A: 101%; **Vitamin C**: 88%; **Calcium**: 13%

Ingredients:

- ☐ 1 pound bok choy, roughly chopped
- ☐ 1/4 cup cashews, toasted
- ☐ 1 onion medium, quartered, sliced
- ☐ 2 1/2 tablespoons sesame oil, dark
- ☐ 2 teaspoons soy sauce, low sodium, gluten-free

Directions:

1. Heat a large skillet over medium-high heat. Pour in the sesame oil.
2. Add in the onions. Cook, stirring for about 1 minutes.
3. Add the bok choy. Stir. Cook for about 1-2 minutes.
4. Pour the soy sauce in and stir. Arrange the bok choy on a serving platter. Top with cashews.

Sautéed Brussels Sprouts with Walnuts

Prep Time: 05 minutes   **Cook Time:** 10 minutes

Serving Size: 137 g **Serves:** 4	
Calories: 160; **Total Fat:** 17 g	
Saturated Fat: 2 g; **Trans Fat:** 0 g	
Protein: 2 g	
Total Carbs: 3 g; **Net Carbs:** 2 g	
Dietary Fiber: 1 g; **Sugars:** <1 g	
Cholesterol: 0 mg; **Sodium:** 190 mg	
Potassium: 80 mg; **Iron:** 4%	
Vitamin A: 0%; **Vitamin C:** 6%; **Calcium:** 2%	

Ingredients:

- ☐ 1 pound Brussels sprouts, very fresh, hard stem and core removed
- ☐ 1/2 cup walnuts, toasted,
- ☐ 2 tablespoons olive oil
- ☐ Generous sprinkling coarse salt and freshly ground black pepper
- ☐ Lemon juice, if desired

Directions:

1. Cut the Brussels sprouts into lengthwise halves. Cut the halves into thin slivers until the sprouts are shredded and they fall apart.
2. Over medium-high heat, heat a heavy skillet; add the olive oil. When the olive oil is shimmering, add

the sprouts; sauté, tossing using tongs, for about 3-4 minutes, or until they turn bright green and start to brown deeply around the edges. Add the walnuts, continue sautéing for 1 minute more. Sprinkle generously with salt and pepper. Is desired, season with lemon juice. Serve.

Zucchini Parmesan

Prep Time: 10 minutes	**Cook Time:** 05 minutes

Serving Size: 114 g   **Serves**: 4

Calories: 93; **Total Fat:** 4 g

Saturated Fat: 1.6 g; **Trans Fat**: 0 g

Protein: 2.4 g

Total Carbs: 4.0 g; **Net Carbs:** 2.9 g

Dietary Fiber: 1.1 g; **Sugars:** 1.9 g

Cholesterol: 3 mg; **Sodium**: 44 mg

Potassium: 266 mg; **Iron:** 2%

Vitamin A: 4%; **Vitamin C**: 30%; **Calcium**: 5%

Ingredients:

- ☐ 2 zucchinis
- ☐ 2 teaspoons parmesan cheese, shredded
- ☐ 2 tablespoons olive oil
- ☐ 2 teaspoons lemon juice
- ☐ 2 teaspoons garlic, minced
- ☐ 1 teaspoon Italian seasoning

Directions:

1. In a lengthwise manner, cut the zucchini from top to bottom into 4 pieces. Cut each lengthwise piece into halves.
2. In a skillet, heat the olive oil over medium heat. Put the zucchini. Cook for about 5 minutes,

turning occasionally, until cooked to desired tenderness or slightly browned on each side. Remove the skillet from the heat.

3. Add in the garlic, lemon juice, and the Italian seasoning. Gently mix. Transfer to a serving dish. Top with the Parmesan cheese.

Crème Chantilly Fried Apples

Prep Time: 05 minutes	**Cook Time:** 10 minutes

Serving Size: 106 g	**Serves:** 3

Calories: 224; **Total Fat:** 20.3 g

Saturated Fat: 12.7 g; **Trans Fat:** 0 g

Protein: 0.9 g

Total Carbs: 10.8 g; **Net Carbs:** 9.2 g

Dietary Fiber: 1.6 g; **Sugars:** 7.7 g

Cholesterol: 67 mg; **Sodium:** 68 mg

Potassium: 94 mg; **Iron:** 2%

Vitamin A: 15%; **Vitamin C:** 8%; **Calcium:** 3%

Ingredients:

- ☐ 1 apple
- ☐ 1 tablespoon Splenda or 1 packet of Stevia
- ☐ 1/4 teaspoon cinnamon
- ☐ 100 ml heavy cream
- ☐ 2 tablespoons butter
- ☐ A pinch real vanilla powder

Directions:

1. Cut the apples into small cubes.
2. Lightly brown the butter in a small skillet. Fry the apple cubes in the butter.
3. Season with the vanilla powder, cinnamon, and the sweetener. Allow to cool.
4. Transfer in a small glass. Top with vanilla whipped cream.

Pork Rind Tortillas

Prep Time: 05 minutes   **Cook Time:** 15 minutes

Serving Size: 131 g **Serves:** 12	
Calories: 332; **Total Fat:** 26 g	
Saturated Fat: 12.8 g; **Trans Fat**: 0 g	
Protein: 22.8 g	
Total Carbs: 2.9 g; **Net Carbs:** 2.9 g	
Dietary Fiber: 0 g; **Sugars:** 0.9 g	
Cholesterol: 287 mg; **Sodium:** 561 mg	
Potassium: 157mg; **Iron:** 12%	
Vitamin A: 16%; **Vitamin C**: 1%; **Calcium:** 7%	

Ingredients:

- ☐ 8 eggs
- ☐ 4 ounces regular or hot and spicy pork rinds
- ☐ 1 package (1 cup) cream cheese, softened
- ☐ 1 tablespoon granulated garlic
- ☐ 1 tablespoon ground cumin
- ☐ 1/3 cup water
- ☐ Olive oil or coconut cooking spray

Directions:

1. Put the pork rinds into the food processor. Process for about 10 seconds until turned to dust.

2. Add the rest of the ingredients into the food processor. Process for about 45 seconds until the mixture turns into a smooth batter.
3. Heat a non-stick skillet over medium-high. Grease with the cooking spray.
4. Pour about 1/3 cup batter into the skillet.
5. With a plastic spatula, gently spread as thin as you can. Cook for about 2 minutes or until golden brown. Flip and continue to cook for about 45 seconds more.
6. Repeat the process with the rest of the batter.
7. Serve with favorite taco toppings (ground beef, salsa, guacamole, baby lettuce, sour cream, shredded cheese.

Cheesy Taco

Prep Time: 05 minutes   **Cook Time:** 15 minutes

Serving Size: 241 g   **Serves:** 6

Calories: 295; **Total Fat:** 14.4 g

Saturated Fat: 7.8 g; **Trans Fat:** 0 g

Protein: 31.7 g

Total Carbs: 8.9 g; **Net Carbs:** 7.1 g

Dietary Fiber: 1.8 g; **Sugars:** 2.9 g

Cholesterol: 97 mg; **Sodium**: 433 mg

Potassium: 629 mg; **Iron:** 85%

Vitamin A: 100%; **Vitamin C**: 129%; **Calcium**: 25%

Ingredients:

- ☐ 1 pound lean ground beef
- ☐ 1 can (10 ounces) diced tomatoes with green chilies
- ☐ 1 large yellow onion, diced
- ☐ 1 ½ cup cheddar and jack cheese, shredded
- ☐ 2 bell peppers, diced
- ☐ 3 cups baby kale/spinach mixture
- ☐ Green onions, to garnish
- ☐ Taco seasoning

Directions:

1. In a skillet, lightly brown the ground beef, crumbling well. Drain excess grease.

2. Add in the onions and the peppers. Cook until browned.
3. Add in the canned tomatoes, and seasoning. Add 1 tablespoon of the tomato liquid or water if need to evenly coat the mixture.
4. Add the kale-spinach mix. Cook until wilted. Mix all of the ingredients well.
5. Cover with the shredded cheese. Let the cheese melt. Serve over cauliflower rice, bed of lettuce, or in tacos.

Roasted Rosemary-Herbed Almonds

Prep Time: 05 minutes   **Cook Time:** 15 minutes

Serving Size: 55 g   **Serves:** 4

Calories: 309; **Total Fat:** 27.2 g

Saturated Fat: 3.9 g; **Trans Fat:** 0 g

Protein: 10.2 g

Total Carbs: 11.3 g; **Net Carbs:** 4.6 g

Dietary Fiber: 6.7 g; **Sugars:** 2 g

Cholesterol: 8 mg; **Sodium:** 1164 mg

Potassium: 366 mg; **Iron:** 13%

Vitamin A: 3%; **Vitamin C:** 2%; **Calcium:** 15%

Ingredients:

- ☐ 2 cups whole almonds, raw, skin-on
- ☐ 2 tablespoons dried rosemary
- ☐ 1 tablespoon ghee
- ☐ 1/4 teaspoon black pepper, freshly ground
- ☐ 2 teaspoons kosher salt

Directions:

1. In a large skillet over medium-low heat, melt the ghee.
2. Put in the nuts, arranging them in a single layer in the skillet. Stir the almonds, coating each with the ghee.
3. Add in the rosemary, salt, and pepper. Taste, and adjust seasoning according to taste.

4. Toast the almonds for about 8-12 minutes, stirring often, until aromatic and darkened.
5. Transfer to a plate. Allow to cool to room temperature. Serve or store in an airtight container for up to 7 days.

Mozzarella Pepperoni Skillet Pizza

Prep Time: 10 minutes **Cook Time:** 20 minutes

Serving Size: 62 g **Serves:** 4

Calories: 196; **Total Fat:** 14.3 g

Saturated Fat: 6.6 g; **Trans Fat:** 0.3 g

Protein: 14.5 g

Total Carbs: 2.8 g; **Net Carbs:** 2.8 g

Dietary Fiber: 0 g; **Sugars:** 0.8 g

Cholesterol: 38 mg; **Sodium:** 526 mg

Potassium: 64 mg; **Iron:** 3%

Vitamin A: 11%; **Vitamin C:** 2%; **Calcium:** 27%

Ingredients:

- 4 ounces mozzarella cheese, or more to cover the bottom of 10-inch skillet
- 12 pepperoni slices
- 1 ounce Parmesan cheese
- 2 tablespoons tomatoes, crushed
- 1 teaspoon garlic powder
- 1 teaspoon Italian seasoning or dried basil
- 1 teaspoon red pepper, crushed
- 1 teaspoon basil, fresh, torn

Directions:

1. Heat a small, non-stick skillet over medium heat.

2. Evenly cover the bottom with the mozzarella cheese. This will serve as the crust.
3. With the back of a spoon, lightly spread the tomatoes over the cheese, leaving a border around the edges of the cheese crust.
4. Sprinkle with the garlic powder and the Italian seasoning or dried basil.
5. Arrange the pepperoni on top. Cook until bubbled, sizzling, and the edges of the crust are brown.
6. With a spatula, try lifting the edges. When done, the pizza will lift easily from the pan. If the pizza still sticks, it means it is not yet done. Lift and check frequently.
7. When the pizza lifts up easily, work the spatula slowly and gently underneath, loosening up the entire pizza. Transfer to a cutting board.
8. Lightly sprinkle with parmesan, basil leaves, and red pepper.
9. Cool for about 5 minutes to allow the crust to firm. Cut with a pizza cutter. Transfer to a serving plate.

Pork Tacos

Prep Time: 10 minutes   **Cook Time:** 30 minutes

Serving Size: 241 g   **Serves:** 4

Calories: 501; **Total Fat:** 26.5 g

Saturated Fat: 10.8 g; **Trans Fat:** 0.1 g

Protein: 55.2 g

Total Carbs: 8.3 g; **Net Carbs:** 8.3 g

Dietary Fiber: 0 g; **Sugars:** 2.5 g

Cholesterol: 166 mg; **Sodium:** 424 mg

Potassium: 770 mg; **Iron:** 16%

Vitamin A: 12%; **Vitamin C:** 0%; **Calcium:** 27%

Ingredients:

- ☐ 3 cups (700 grams) pork mince
- ☐ 4 romaine lettuce leaves
- ☐ 3 teaspoons taco seasoning
- ☐ 1/2 cup goat cheese
- ☐ 1/2 cup mayonnaise

Directions:

1. Put the pork mince in a skillet. Cook for about 20 minutes until brown. Remove the skillet from the heat. Allow the meat to cool.
2. Take a lettuce leaf. Put 1/4 of the pork mince in the center of the leaf. Season with the taco seasoning. Place 1/8 cup of the goat cheese and a dollop of the mayonnaise. Wrap the leaf securely.

Chicken Tofu Nuggets with Spicy Dip

Prep Time: 6 hours, 5 minutes   **Cook Time:** 15 minutes

Serving Size: 340 g **Serves:** 3	
Calories: 394; **Total Fat:** 31.9 g	
Saturated Fat: 8.6 g; **Trans Fat:** 0 g	
Protein: 21.5 g	
Total Carbs: 10.8 g; **Net Carbs:** 6.3 g	
Dietary Fiber: 4.5 g; **Sugars:** 2 g	
Cholesterol: 0 mg; **Sodium:** 1304 mg	
Potassium: 616 mg; **Iron:** 39%	
Vitamin A: 3%; **Vitamin C:** 3%; **Calcium:** 25%	

Ingredients:

- [ ] 3 tablespoons nutritional yeast
- [ ] 2 cups chicken-flavored vegan broth (double strength)
- [ ] 1/4 cup vegetable oil
- [ ] 1/2 teaspoon onion, dried, minced
- [ ] 1/2 teaspoon garlic, dried
- [ ] 1/2 teaspoon cayenne pepper
- [ ] 1/2 teaspoon black pepper, freshly ground
- [ ] 1/2 cup coconut flour
- [ ] 1 teaspoon salt
- [ ] 1 teaspoon poultry seasoning
- [ ] 1 package (2 cups) tofu, extra-firm; drain, freeze, and then thaw

For the Sriracha mayo:
- ☐ 1/4 cup veganaise or tofu mayo
- ☐ A squeeze of Sriracha, or more according to taste

Directions:
1. Cut the tofu into cubes. Place in a pan. Pout the broth over, making sure it covers the tofu. Refrigerate and let soak for a couple of hours or overnight.
2. Meanwhile, make the Sriracha mayo. Combine the all of the ingredients for the mayo. Add more Sriracha, if desired.
3. When the tofu is marinated, stir together the flour, yeast, spices, salt, and pepper.
4. In a large skillet, heat the vegetable oil on medium-low.
5. Remove the tofu from the broth marinade. Getting a few tofu cubes, toss into the flour mixture, coating the cubes completely.
6. Gently put the coated tofu in the hot oil. Cook until each side for about 2 to 3 minutes or until all sides are browned and crisp. When cooked, place on a wire rack over a paper towel to catch the oil drip. Immediately serve with the Sriracha mayo.

Chocolate Butter Cookie

Prep Time: 30 minutes	**Cook Time:** 30 minutes

Serving Size: 38 g **Serves:** 12
Calories: 198; **Total Fat:** 16.8 g
Saturated Fat: 6.1 g; **Trans Fat**: 0 g
Protein: 4.7 g
Total Carbs: 9.5 g; **Net Carbs:** 6.3 g
Dietary Fiber: 3.2 g; **Sugars:** 4.8 g
Cholesterol: 36 mg; **Sodium**: 139 mg
Potassium: 182 mg; **Iron**: 7%
Vitamin A: 5%; **Vitamin C**: 0%; **Calcium**: 5%

Ingredients:

- ☐ 1 large egg
- ☐ 1 teaspoon pure vanilla extract
- ☐ 1/2 cup butter (or your spread of choice)
- ☐ 1/2 cup chocolate chips, sugar free
- ☐ 1/2 teaspoon sea salt
- ☐ 1/4 cup Splenda or natural granulated sweetener
- ☐ 2 cups almond flour
- ☐ 2 tablespoons coconut sugar

Directions:

1. Preheat the oven to 350F or 176C.
2. In a 9-inch cast iron skillet, heat the butter until bubbling. Reduce the heat to low. Cover pan. Cook

the butter, stirring occasionally, until it starts to brown. When brown, remove the skillet from the heat. Allow to cool for about 5 minutes.

3. Meanwhile, whisk the eggs and the vanilla extract together. Add in the coconut sugar and the sweetener. Whisk together until combined. When the butter is cool, add into the egg mixture. Combine well.

4. Sift in the almond flour, pressing any lumps gently over the sieve. Add in the salt and half of the chocolate chips. Mix gently until the batter is creamy. Spoon batter into the skillet. Top with the remaining chocolate chips.

5. Bake for about 25-30 minutes or until the top is set and a toothpick comes out clean when inserted into the center. Serve with frozen yogurt or sugar-free ice cream.

Lasagna Rolls

Prep Time: 25 minutes   **Cook Time:** 20 minutes

Serving Size: 88 g   **Serves:** 8-12

Calories: 149; **Total Fat:** 11.14 g

Saturated Fat: 2.3 g; **Trans Fat:** 0 g

Protein: 4.2 g

Total Carbs: 10.9 g; **Net Carbs:** 8.5 g

Dietary Fiber: 2.4 g; **Sugars:** 3 g

Cholesterol: 1 mg; **Sodium:** 156 mg

Potassium: 294mg; **Iron:** 9%

Vitamin A: 2%; **Vitamin C:** 7%; **Calcium:** 2%

Ingredients:
Rolls:
- ☐ 1 zucchini
- ☐ 1 eggplant
- ☐ 1/2 cup tomato sauce, organic
- ☐ 1 cup cashew cheese (recipe below)
- ☐ 1 teaspoon ghee, coconut oil or sustainable palm oil
- ☐ Salt and pepper to taste

For the cashew cheese:
- ☐ 1 cup raw cashews
- ☐ Water, enough to cover the cashews
- ☐ Sprinkle of sea salt

- [ ] 1/2 tsp garlic powder
- [ ] 1/2 tsp salt

Directions:
For the cashew cheese:
1. Soak the cashews in water and the sea salt for about 8-24 hours. Soaking them overnight is better.
2. Put the soaked cashews into a food processor. Add in the garlic powder and the salt. Blend until the mixture is creamy. If desired, add a little more water to make the mixture thinner. Store in a jar and refrigerate.

For lasagna bites:
1. In a lengthwise manner, slice the zucchini and the eggplant into thin pieces.
2. Sprinkle one side of the slices with salt. With the salted side down, place each side down on a paper towel. Sprinkle the top side with salt. Allow to sit for 10 minutes, allowing the water to be drawn out.
3. With another piece of paper towel, dab the moisture off the zucchini and eggplant slices until dry.
4. In a skillet over high heat, pour the oil and heat. When hot, add the zucchini and the eggplant slices. Cook for about 1-2 minutes per side, until slightly brown and cooked.
5. Once all of the slices are cooked, take 1 slice and put about 1 tablespoon of the cashew cheese in the

middle of the slice. Fold the slice and place on a plate. You can also wrap the cashew cheese with 1 eggplant and 1 zucchini slice together. Repeat the process until all the slices are wrapped with cheese.

6. When all rolls are made, drizzle 1 teaspoon of tomato sauce over each roll. Sprinkle with salt, pepper, and herbs to taste. Serve.

Conclusion

Thank you again for downloading this book. I hope that the recipes help you stay on the Ketogenic Diet!

Finally, if you enjoyed this book I'd like to ask you to leave a review for my book on Amazon, it would be greatly appreciated!

I am constantly looking for way to improve my content to give readers the best value, so if you didn't like the book, I would like to also hear from you:

Twitter: @JeremyStoneEat

Email: Elevatecan@gmail.com

Thank you and good luck!

36470543R00075

Made in the USA
Middletown, DE
02 November 2016